MW00399766

Special Invitation

Please consider attending one of our Exponential 2019 conferences. Exponential's goal is to help shape your paradigm for multiplication, inspire and encourage you to multiply, and equip you to turn ideas into action.

2019 Theme: Made for More: Mobilizing God's People, God's Way

Locations and dates:

Exponential 2019 is our national event, which includes thousands of church multiplication leaders, 150+ Nationally known speakers (including J.D. Greear, Dave Ferguson, Alan Hirsch, Cynthia Marshall and Albert Tate), 200+ Workshops and 15 pre-conference sessions.

2019 National Event: March 4 – 7, 2019 Orlando, FL

Our Exponential regional events are shorter and geographically based (translating to lower overall costs for large teams). Regionals bring the full "punch" of the national conferences' five main stage sessions without the breakout workshops.

2019 Regional Events
Boise, ID, Washington, D.C., Southern CA, Bay Area, CA, Chicago, IL, Houston, TX, and New York City, NY

For more information, please go to exponential.org/events.

Made for More Resources

For information about the 2019 Made for More theme and other FREE Made for More Resources, please visit our Made for More Resource Page.

CHURCH DIFFERENT

UNLEASHING THE CHURCH TO CHANGE THE WORLD

RON DOTZLER

DEDICATION

This book is dedicated to the innovative, pioneering and risk-taking team of leaders that tirelessly and relentlessly helped turn the concepts behind this book into reality.

Thank you, Pastor Josh Dotzler, my son, for leading the charge in building Bridge Church these past several years—without your leadership, many of these concepts wouldn't have become reality. Special thanks to other team members, including my wife, Twany, Pastor Myron Pierce and Shawn Deane. Your innovative and inspiring dedication has powerfully resulted in a different expression of church that is reaching people far from Christ and impacting a broken world.

". . . these who have turned
the world upside down . . ."

Acts 17:6 (NKJV)

CONTENTS

INTRODUCTION

SOMETHING HAD TO CHANGE

I didn't know how I'd make it through the funeral.

All eyes focused on me—the pastor. My insides churned with emotion. What could I say to bring comfort? How could I explain the injustice? Little girls weren't supposed to be brutally murdered.

Seeing the lifeless bodies inside the two small caskets knifed my heart. Freckles smattered Carissa's face while Chloe's lips turned into the hint of a smile. Red roses lined their sides and notes written in crayons rested on their blue print dresses. Their mother wanted me to speak, yet there were no words.

Carissa and Chloe, my two young daughters' best friends, were gone. Tears rolled down my girls' faces when I told them Care Bear and Chloe were up in heaven with Jesus.

I knew the girls' bodies were suitcases housing both spirit and soul, but the finality of life weighted me. Anger flared inside me. The injustice stirred up holy discontent which awakened deep passion. My heart ached over the emptiness, brokenness and injustice around me.

Ron? I heard God call my name. *Could you give your life to this community so other kids won't have their lives cut short by violence?*

As I stood in front of those two small caskets, the reality of crime, violence and death took its toll. I knew something had to change. I couldn't keep doing church the same way while my neighbors died around me. I needed to change the way I led my church.

I needed to do *church different.*

THE CHURCH IS IN DEEP TROUBLE

The impact of the church in America is in serious decline.

Troubling signs appear at every juncture. David T. Olson, author of *The American Church in Crisis* researched data from over 200,000 churches and concluded that "the conditions that produce growth are simply not present. If present trends continue, the church will fall farther behind population growth."[1]

Church researcher and president/CEO of LifeWay Christian Resources, Thom Rainer, describes the state of the American church based on his years of consulting with many different churches and denominations. He writes, "Eight out of ten of the approximately 400,000 churches in the United States are declining or have plateaued."[2]

According to the Barna Group, church attendance and impressions of the church are the lowest in recent history and most drastic among millennials.

- Only 2 in 10 Americans under 30 believe attending a church is important or worthwhile (an all-time low).
- 59% of millennials raised in a church have dropped out.
- 35% of millennials have an *anti-church* stance, believing the church does more harm than good.
- Millennials are the least likely age group of anyone to attend church.[3]

The lost, hurting and confused are no longer looking to the church for answers to life's most pressing questions.

While it's true that non-Christians aren't looking to the church, even more disheartening, however, is that many churches aren't looking for non-Christians. Churches are not connecting with or reaching lost people; we're simply reproducing a church model that is failing to reach people far from Christ.

My heart is saddened to hear the church is struggling when the church is God's answer to those who are desperate. However, a hope-filled future awaits if we will make significant changes that will reawaken our churches to our salvation-focused, world-changing mandate.

> A hope-filled future awaits if we will make significant changes that will reawaken our churches to our salvation-focused, world-changing mandate.

A FAULTY CHURCH MODEL

Many years ago, I attended a conference hosted by a prominent church. The helpful workshops left me excited to implement all I'd learned when I returned home. Without warning, one of the speakers from Europe shocked me when he predicted a sharp decline in attendance of the North American church. His announcement left me reeling.

I leaned back in my chair, trying to process his statement. *Why did this pastor have such a grim view of the church? How could he be so bold as to make such a negative futuristic claim?*

Without missing a beat, the pastor asked a very intriguing question: why had the church in Europe died, no longer exerting influence in society? With no real answers from the audience, he explained how the church in Europe had a faulty church model which the States inherited.

The culture in Europe shifted away from God, and the church lost sight of those outside the walls and focused only on its members. This faulty model had a single-minded focus and emphasis on discipling believers, and therefore incomplete in its ability to reach and receive lost people. If the church in North America didn't make changes, he claimed, it would soon mirror European church—empty, lifeless and no longer relevant.

My heart sank. I didn't want to believe his disheartening view. Yet his projection stuck with me, pressing me to work against the tide when I saw his prediction coming true.

SOCIAL INFLUENCE FOR SPIRITUAL IMPACT

During these challenging moments of reflection, I began to realize the spiritual impact a church had on unbelievers tied directly to social influence. In other words, if pastors and leaders didn't have social influence in their community, they wouldn't have much of a spiritual impact. Social influence was a huge key to reaching people far from Christ.

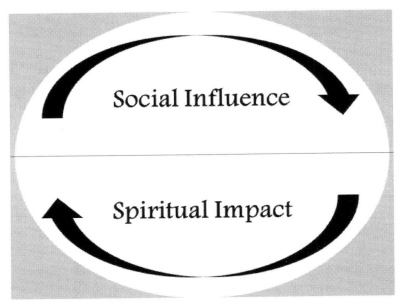

In my previous church plants, I had discipleship plans for our members. New classes, Bible studies, sermons and an array of teaching dominated my work as a pastor. But how much did I intentionally reach and disciple unbelievers?

Honestly, very little.

When I proposed the idea of changing our church model to include social influence for spiritual impact, several pastors repeated the same sentiment. *Ron, I love the idea of reaching our city for Christ. But please know, my church pays me to take care of them.*

There it was.

Pastors and church staff are primarily hired and paid to *tend* to their congregation. Putting time, energy and resources into hiring staff to focus on gaining social influence for spiritual impact is not even a blip on the radar. Sadly, as churches lose social influence, they lose credibility and relevance in their communities. Without social influence, spiritual impact will diminish.

STAGNATION

Jesus came to save lost people. Born the *savior* of the world, he died on a cross for the *sinfulness of mankind.* Jesus "came to seek and to save the lost." Luke 19:10 (NIV) If unbelievers matter that much to Christ, they should matter that much to me.

Somehow, I had missed the point.

Despite a great amount of zeal and sincerity to plant churches, my first four attempts at planting churches reflected this faulty, incomplete model. The absence of conversion growth—reaching unbelievers and connecting them to a church family—left all four churches stagnant within three years.

I pastored for years, but never really focused on how best to reach lost people. I had great intentions to extend, but because I had no emphasis in social influence, I didn't fully understand unbelievers. As a result, my insensitive and irrelevant approach fell short. Everything from community outreaches to Sunday morning services focused on the seemingly polished lives of my believing friends rather than meeting my nonbelieving neighbors in the messy places of their lives.

My attempts to reach the lost weren't as central to the heart of my church as I had thought. I got so caught up in preaching, teaching and caring for the members that I unknowingly missed the rest of the world around me. At best, outreaches were one-time events unconnected to the normal rhythms of church life. Without new growth, stagnation loomed.

After working with many pastors and church leadership teams over the years, I've discovered many churches in America mirror my first church plants. As social influence wanes, spiritual impact wanes. I believe in the incredible power and potential of the local church to reach a lost and broken world, but I also know the hard facts—the church in America is experiencing significant decline in influence and in attendance.

EXTENDING

Extending to unbelievers in the New Testament church produced powerful results. Being present and active in the community demonstrates Christ's love to an unbelieving world. *When the church takes interest in the community, the community takes interest in the church.*

When the church takes interest in the community, the community takes interest in the church.

Extending was the piece of the model I'd been missing. I preached the need to witness from the pulpit and encouraged my congregation to impact their mission field, but the seats didn't fill with nonbelievers. The issue boiled down to leadership. I didn't provide consistent opportunities for extending or prepare my congregation to invite their unbelieving friends, co-workers and neighbors into their lives, so fear gripped them.

I *tended* my church well. I preached, taught and cared for my congregation, but I didn't provide the leadership to consistently *extend* the members beyond the walls to unbelievers. Not only did we fail to connect with people outside the walls of the church, the occasional unbelieving guest didn't return because my Sunday services catered to the believer.

I prided myself for doing outreaches, but really, most activities kept me and my congregation inside the walls of the church focused on ourselves. I didn't make any significant changes in my approach to doing church to make the unbeliever feel welcomed enough to return the following week.

If I wanted to build a church that both *tended* and *extended* to nonbelievers, it became apparent I had to do *church different.*

Vibrant, growing churches not only focus on believers, they also focus on unbelievers. With this new understanding, I had to include *extending* into my church model by appointing staff and resources intentionally focused on social influence for spiritual impact. Extending my congregation beyond the walls of the church to impact the community and connect with unbelievers was no longer an option.

> Vibrant, growing churches not only focus on believers, they also focus on unbelievers.

Fortunately, I'm not the only one talking about this. My friends at Exponential have spent considerable time thinking about this and articulating the importance of mobilizing what they call everyday missionaries to carry the fullness of Jesus—His living water—beyond church walls and into a parched world. They're talking about what I'm talking about: revolutionary change. I like the way they say it:

"Revolutionary change will be less about fueling the capacity of the local church and more about releasing and mobilizing the sending capacity of the church into every crack and cranny of society."

They have even verbally expressed what it will take to extend the local church. My good friend and Exponential CEO Todd Wilson has boiled it down to what he calls a flywheel: Disciple-making churches sending out everyday missionaries who will start new gatherings and churches of disciple makers that ultimately, birth a new flywheel, starting the cycle all over again. Check out the illustration below:

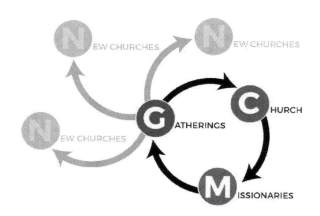

Throughout this book, you'll hear me referring to some of the frameworks, principles and shifts that Exponential has worked hard to identify and help churches like mine mobilize people to become the church God has designed. Churches full of disciples who are joyfully living out their calling to make disciples wherever they are. Jesus' words are so true for all of us: "The thief does not come except to steal, and to kill, and to destroy. I have come that they may have life, and that they may have it more abundantly." (John 10:10, NKJV)

REACHING UNBELIEVERS

I love the local *extending* church. While all of eternity hangs in the balance, God still sees his beautiful bride, the church, as carriers of his salvation message to a broken, lost and hurting world. The king of the universe really wants to use churches like yours and mine. Despite its imperfect earthly form, the local church is the hope of the world.

Since our official launch in October 2008, Bridge Church—my fifth church plant—has incorporated *extending* into our church model and has grown from 12 founding members to over 700 people who regularly attend Sunday morning services. Our leadership focus expanded to include loving people outside the church walls, building a culture of hope on Sunday mornings, and shaping the faith of our members through an experience-rich discipleship process. As a result, people far from Christ are experiencing radical conversion and growing deeper in their relationship with Christ. Conversion growth is the desired outcome of an extending church and must be central to everything we, as pastors, church leaders and Christians do.

Many governmental entities, including the police, the mayor and the governor, have recognized the significant difference and impact Bridge Church is making in our city. God is truly transforming broken lives in a powerful way and impacting neighborhoods, communities and the city.

Throughout this book, I interchange the terms *nonbelievers, non-Christian, lost, unchurched* and *people far from Christ* to refer to unbelievers who have yet to become followers of Jesus.

While Bridge is located in the inner city, the principles referenced in this book are transferable to both rural and suburban areas. Our leadership team has worked with many churches to be more intentional about *extending* into their respective communities. This includes a range of churches from small-town rural areas to large suburban churches in both the United States and Mexico.

The goal of this book is to unleash your church to change the world. Jesus' heart breaks for the hopelessness which surrounds us. Lives are on the line, and it's incumbent upon us, as pastors, leaders and Christians, to reconnect with the lost in our city. We must live with a sense of urgency for the countless lives trapped in darkness, waiting for the hope we need to share.

What got us here won't get us there. It's time to change.

Like never before, we have to be and do **church different**.

SECTION I:
DEMONSTRATE LOVE

1

THE REVELATION THAT CHANGED EVERYTHING

LESSON FROM A DRUG DEALER

My son and I spent hours on our driveway court, so we loved to challenge kids in the neighborhood to a basketball game. When Diamond and his friends rolled slowly through the neighborhood in his sporty Chrysler 180, bass thumping, I invited them to shoot some hoops.

Diamond looked amused. "I'll play you, old man." He swaggered toward me carrying a brown bag of liquor. One of his friends joined us while the other leaned against the low rider.

"Loser buys the winner a soda and a candy bar," I dared him.

Diamond grinned, a gold tooth showing. He counted on a win, clueless to the skills of my nine-year-old or my days playing basketball in college.

Every shot brought smack talk from Diamond's friend. "You're letting a little boy and an old man beat you."

Diamond cursed, clearly impressed. Our win brought a smile of respect across his face.

"Tomorrow, old man. Tomorrow." He promised to be back.

Diamond showed up at our house every day for the next six weeks. As we played basketball, I couldn't help but be impressed with the strong bonds he had formed in the community. His influence extended throughout the neighborhood because of his relational savvy. Even while we played basketball, little kids would come up and high five Diamond. Intentions far from moral, he built relationships with kids, buying them bikes or giving them money so they would do his drug runs or protect his territory.

I learned a valuable lesson from my drug-dealing neighbor. Like Diamond, I needed to be as relational and intentional with my neighbors if I wanted to influence them for God's kingdom.

In a moment of honesty, I had to ask myself: Was I willing to invest my time and my heart to develop the depth of relationships like Diamond had grown over the years? How far would I go to reach my neighbors for a much greater cause?

DISILLUSIONED

As a new believer in my early twenties, I shared my faith easily and at every opportunity. I fell in love with Jesus, and I wanted to tell everyone about my newfound hope. I didn't know a lot about the Bible, but what little I knew, I shared.

The more I hung out with Christians, the greater my distance grew with the unchurched. My church discipled me on how to have a *personal relationship* with

Jesus through prayer, Bible studies, sermons and other classroom-oriented training. While helpful, I wasn't discipled in my *purposeful relationship* with Jesus, where I effectively demonstrated and communicated God's love to a lost and broken world.

As church leaders, it's easy to become consumed with *tending* to and caring for church members. Without providing the critical leadership structure and systems to help people grow in their *purposeful relationship* with Jesus, reaching lost people becomes less and less a reality.

Sadly, the more time I spent at church, the less I shared my faith. Eventually, I became disillusioned with unbelievers and their ungodly ways and became more and more critical and judgmental. This downward spiral in my heart resulted from a continual emphasis on knowing biblical truth in order to defend morality and debate with unbelievers. Rather than allow God's truth to change me, I was determined to change others. While my head grew in biblical knowledge, my heart shrunk in empathy and compassion for others. I lacked love and grace.

This hardness of my heart, and a distant life in the suburbs, isolated me from the harsh reality of many in my city. When I read newspaper articles about murder and crime in the inner city, I critically judged *those people* for their irresponsibility and blamed *them* for what they should or should not be doing. In my negative view, I thought *they* deserved the mess of problems they experienced.

Because of my cynicism, the distance between me and *them* left me unmoved and unaffected. Quite sadly, I felt no compassion, empathy or concern. I was clueless and unconcerned to the conditions impacting a large population of children, youth and families.

In my quest for truth and holiness, I forgot love and grace. My heart became cold toward those far from Christ. My constant emphasis on my *personal relationship* with Jesus moved me inward rather than outward toward loving others.

I somehow had become a Pharisee—religious.

Yikes.

THE REVELATION: LOVE-HOPE-FAITH

The inner city wrecked me.

I left my job as an engineer and my comfortable life in the suburbs for a life I never fathomed for me and my young family.

I thought God would send me overseas as a missionary, but he broke my heart and stirred me to compassion for my new neighbors instead. I hurt for them and wanted to share my hope. In an attempt to connect with my neighbors, I hosted block parties. However, as I tried to share my faith, I came off as harsh and confrontational. My heart was sincere, but my neighbors looked at me like I'd come from a different planet. Diamond made it look so easy, compared with my awkward, insensitive, clueless approach to reaching my unchurched neighbors.

Desperate, I asked God for revelation. He led me to 1 Corinthians 13:13. "And now these three remain: faith, hope and love. But the greatest of these is love."

"Love?" I exclaimed. "Why love?"

I must've read the passage about faith, hope and love a thousand times, but this particular morning, a question popped off the page. Why did God consider love the greatest of these? Surely faith was the answer. After all, didn't the book of Hebrews say it was impossible to please God *without faith*? And then Ephesians 2 echoes, "we are saved by grace *through faith*." Or what about the passage in Mark 8:36 which read, "For what will it profit a man if he gains the whole world, and *loses his soul?*" (NKJV) Surely faith—not love—had to be the most important. I prayed and wrestled with this passage for two weeks to understand what God meant.

"Lord, I don't get this," I cried out, and He finally answered.

Ron, when you received me by **faith**, *didn't you get a* **hope** *like never before that your life could be different?*

I nodded in answer to the question which filled my spirit.

Doesn't that **hope** *translate into actions of* **love**, *making love the ultimate expression of your faith?*

"Wow. Thank you, Lord," I thought. "I like that."

It's as if those three words merged into one word where faith, hope and love came together. No longer was my faith separate and distinct from hope and love. My faith had elements of hope and love. The faith I carried could actually be *hopeful* and *expressed in love* toward others.

> The faith I carried could actually be *hopeful* and *expressed in love* toward others.

The Lord spoke again. *Think back to the years before you became a Christ-follower. Didn't "love" draw you to me? Didn't the loving actions and encouraging words from other Christians give you a sense of "hope" that life could be different? As a result, didn't that hope lead you to receive me by "faith?"*

The revelation knocked the spiritual wind out of me. As a Christ-follower, my faith gave me hope like I'd never known before which resulted in actions of love toward others. Before I chose to follow Jesus, however, seeing the loving actions of Christians gave me a vision of hope which resulted in steps of faith toward a life with Christ.

I'd never considered the complementary principles of *faith—hope—love* and *love—hope—faith*. For the Christ-follower, the movement progressed from faith, to hope, to love. Whereas, for the non-Christ-follower, the movement flowed in the reverse, from love, to hope, to faith. Just as love is the ultimate expression of our faith, faith is the ultimate acceptance of His love.

> Just as love is the ultimate expression of our faith, faith is the ultimate acceptance of His love.

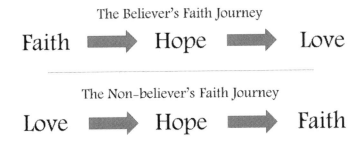

The Believer's Faith Journey

Faith ⟹ Hope ⟹ Love

The Non-believer's Faith Journey

Love ⟹ Hope ⟹ Faith

As I reflected on this newfound revelation, God continued to give me insight.

I know you love me, Ron, but you've been trying to reach unbelievers for me based on **faith**. God paused as the words took meaning.

Stop reaching them based on **faith** *and focus on* **love***. Love people, Ron. Engage them with love. You don't have to save people. I will draw all men to myself. When they ask questions, simply be prepared to give an answer for the hope that lies within you. I will draw them to myself and save them.*

As I considered my own faith journey, I realized my faith in Christ began with love. I didn't automatically come to Christ because someone shared the gospel with me. My brother and Christian friends in college first loved and valued me. I saw the excitement and hope with which they lived their lives. This hope led me to begin asking questions of faith. Ultimately, I accepted Jesus as my savior when they answered my questions by sharing the gospel.

As a Christian, this equation reversed. My newfound faith in Jesus gave me a hope that my life had meaning, and my future looked bright. This hope filled me with joy and excitement and resulted in expressions of love toward others.

This new revelation forever changed my understanding of the power of the local church and its capacity to reach lost people. I not only experienced a new personal freedom to love people without expectations and condemnation, this insight changed the way I led and positioned our church to reach people far from Christ.

Galatians 5:6b says, "The only thing that counts is faith expressing itself through love." (NIV) We simply need to love people. God will draw, save and change them—not us. Both as individuals and together as the church, our place is not to judge or change unchurched people. Jesus does all of that. Our job is to simply love people and receive them with open arms, always ready to give an answer for the hope that lies within us. (1 Peter 3:15)

> We simply need to love people.
> God will draw, save and change them—not us.

THE POWER OF LOVE

The longer I lived as a Christian, the fewer relationships I had with nonbelievers. My best friends were other Christians. Not only did we have small groups and Bible studies in common, we spent all our free time together.

Moving into the inner city showed me how few unbelievers I really knew—much less befriended.

Meeting Diamond and others in my new community shifted my paradigm. Combined with this new love-hope-faith revelation, I had a new freedom to love people right where they were—without condemnation.

Love welled inside of me for lost people. I no longer had to worry about the clash of my lifestyle with the unbeliever. I didn't have to share the gospel in a canned process. Love brought new freedom.

For example, after leading a team of volunteers in cleaning up an abandoned property, my staff and I returned the next morning to a complete mess. Shattered glass from the new windows we'd installed littered the floor while concrete mix dusted the entire site. Our tools were gone.

When we found out a local gang was responsible, my staff wanted to call the cops, but I challenged them to do something different. Rather than press charges, I suggested we get to know the young men and even take them out to eat. In hearing this, one of my employees exploded. Having been through this before, he wanted justice, not another mess to clean up. After a lively discussion with the entire staff, we closed our time in prayer, asking God to give us his heart for the situation.

Later that day, God used the very same staff member to invite the young men out for burgers. The connection and display of unconditional love was powerful. A week later, our team again invited them to join us for pizza, and we got to know the young men better.

I can still see the dumbfounded look of shock on their faces at the invitation. Either we were crazy, or we had something worth pursuing.

The young men expected retaliation; instead we showed love—the only power that can transform a life. Instead of stealing from us, the gang members began to respect our desire to clean up the neighborhood. From that point forward, we never had another incident. They went from taking and destroying our property to protecting it.

Intentionally loving people, no matter the situation or circumstance, is powerful. When our lifestyle reflects the life and love of Jesus, we are moved to make a difference when we see the chaos, confusion and craziness around us. We fulfill our calling to bring God's heavenly kingdom on earth by loving others no matter the circumstances.

That's the power of love.

BECOMING RELEVANT
TO THE UNCHURCHED

Dear Christian,

I've been wanting to write this letter for a long time, but I wasn't sure talking to you would do any good. Like you, I'm on my own journey.

I've been very frustrated because it feels like you don't even listen to me. Do you really care what I think or feel? I know there has to be more to life, but everywhere I turn, I face another roadblock. I'm struggling at work. The bills keep piling up. My kids are hanging with the wrong crowd, and my mom just got diagnosed with cancer. I really just want to find peace.

I'm looking for genuine love and acceptance, not spiritual answers.

You talk about truth and scripture in such a way that seems like you're shoving your opinion down my throat. I often feel judged by you because I don't understand your thinking. If you knew the things I've done, would you accept me? Will I ever measure up to your standard? You have a different perspective that sounds so foreign. When I'm around you, will you make me feel valued and loved anyway?

I just want to be happy. I'm not searching for some lofty hope or someone's view of truth.

To be honest, your religion seems to make you angry all the time. It's a real downer when you point out everything you find to be wrong in this world. You seem so against everything, it's hard to believe you could really have my best interest in mind. Your complaints don't exactly inspire me to become a Christian like you. If you could just smile and laugh, your joy would attract me.

Before you talk to me about my spiritual needs, I want to know you care for me.

Life is tough. Many times, I feel empty and lonely. I've been put down and excluded. When I'm struggling, and you say, "Jesus is the answer," your simple statements ring hollow. I don't want to be around people who are always judging me or trying to set me straight. What I really want to know is if you care about me as a friend. I need real friends. Friends who stand by me when I'm alone, afraid, or hurt. If you want to influence me, just be my friend.

Sincerely,

Your non-Christian neighbor

BROKENNESS LEADS TO URGENCY

This letter breaks my heart because, in many ways, I was that Christian.

Too consumed with my church family, I didn't spend much time with those outside the church. As a result, I stood on the sidelines pointing out the problems in our world. I had plenty of answers, but very little empathy.

Most days, non-Christians weren't even on my radar. At best, my conversations with them were awkward. I knew I should share Jesus with others, but I had lost touch with anyone not in the church. I had built a cocoon around me that sealed me off from non-Christians.

Never was this more evident than when I left the safety of the suburbs to live in the inner city over 30 years ago. Until I stared into the faces of brokenness and hopelessness, the deepest cries of my city left me unmoved and unresponsive.

The inner-city statistics were alarming. High crime, violence and murder seemed normal. Poor education, high unemployment, dilapidated houses and unkept lawns left little to be desired.

The first time I saw my neighbors across the street, a man ran out of the house yelling and carrying a machete while another man chased him with a pitchfork. The police visited my new neighbors more times in one week than I'd seen their presence in all my years living in the suburbs. In a strange combination, an abundance of drug addicts, prostitutes and gang members lived alongside laborers, daycare providers and teachers who made up my block.

The dysfunction was like nothing I'd ever experienced. The constant gunfire, crime, violence and poverty took on new meaning when I began to meet my neighbors.

One particularly sobering newspaper article reported that 31 shootings happened within the time span of a single summer month. As I stared at the pictured faces and saw the listed addresses—houses to my left and to my right—God's heart for the brokenness around me swelled inside of me. My neighbors were dying around me despite all my years living and working in the inner city.

The inner city was no longer a distant, faceless community. The daily trauma awakened me to the pain God felt and increased my empathy. God moved beyond getting my attention to grabbing my affection for my hurting neighbors.

FIRST ATTEMPT AT OUTREACH

Before connecting with Diamond and others in my new community, I attempted to engage the unchurched through outreaches. But I didn't understand love-hope-faith, so I missed a crucial element.

Love.

My outreaches were *faith-based*. Not *love-based*. As a result, my outreaches fell short.

Pathetically short.

A group of friends volunteered to help me invite my new neighbors to an afternoon of games and free food at my first block party. Three hundred people showed up as the smell of hot dogs and hamburgers on the grill filled the air, and a Christian worship band played music in the background. Toward the end, I took a stand on a makeshift pulpit and shared the gospel message of how my neighbors could have everlasting life. Believing the day a success, my friends and I made plans to host another block party.

A few weeks later, only 200 people showed up to the same event. Sadly, the head count dwindled to 100 people the following month. Discouraged, I asked pastor friends for advice. None of them questioned my tactics; in fact, they applauded my courageous and bold approach. They blamed my audience. People were the problem. Today's culture didn't care about the things of Christ.

Despite my admirable intentions, my approach backfired. I tried to persuade my audience to change, but they were far from convinced.

I tried to *faith* people to Jesus rather than simply *love* them and trust Jesus to do the rest. My lack of success came from attempting to *convince* people with the truth rather than *compel* them with Christ's love.

I resigned myself to failure and gave up doing outreaches until years later.

INCREASING OUR CULTURAL IQ

American culture once closely mirrored the values of the Christian church. Church was central to life. Prayer in schools was common, and courthouses around the country featured the Ten Commandments. Because the surrounding culture had a *God consciousness,* churches could more easily open their doors and attract people. While this may have been effective years ago, churches no longer experience the benefit of a Christian-friendly culture.

Our 21st century culture no longer prioritizes the Sabbath, Christian holidays and traditions. Americans overall don't connect with the things of God as they once did.

The Pew Research Center notes the number of Americans who do not identify with any religion has grown to more than 13 million self-identified atheists and agnostics, as well as nearly 33 million more who claim no particular religion. Unaffiliated is now the second largest religious demographic in America.[4]

That bears out in what my friends at Exponential have discovered. When they set out to identify what they call Level 5 rapidly multiplying churches here in the States, they found less than .005%. In fact, less than 4% are reproducing (Level 4). The majority (80% to 90%) of U.S. churches are not reproducing and are either in attendance decline or plateaued (Levels 1 and 2).

Further, the average age of a Christian in America is 49 years old. Twenty-one percent are 65 or older.[5] In 1958, according to Gallup, 92% of Americans identified as Christians while only 2% said they had no religion. In 2017, almost 60 years later, 59% of Americans identified as Christians while 20% said they had no religion. Where 59% of Baby Boomers (born 1946-64) say religion is "very important" in their lives, only 38% of younger Millennials (born 1990-96) agree.[6] Without an influx of new believers, the church will eventually grow old and die.

As pastors and leaders, we can be like the men of Issachar "who understood the times and knew what Israel should do." (1 Chronicles 12:32 NIV) Increasing our cultural IQ is critical to understanding how best to engage and impact our surrounding community. Knowing the mind, spirit and essence of our culture is essential if we're going to communicate the gospel effectively. Just like a mechanic must first diagnose the problem before he can repair a car, so we also must first diagnose our surrounding culture so that we can wisely know what we should do to engage and impact unchurched people with the good news of Jesus Christ.

We must become community experts to reach unchurched people. Surveys and interviews are a great start. Years ago, the police surveyed inner city residents in Omaha to discover the most pressing concerns. Rather than gangs, drugs, and violence—the expected answers, stray dogs, abandoned cars, and backed-up sewer problems bothered the community. Police thought they understood the concerns UNTIL they actually spoke with the residents. We need face-to-face conversations in our quest to become proficient in understanding the unchurched. Then we can use the information we learn to meaningfully connect with unbelievers.

Because our surrounding American culture is shifting in dramatic ways, we must act sensitively and genuinely in the way we connect with people and introduce them to the good news of Jesus. Therefore, as leaders, we not only need to increase our cultural IQ, we need to love the unchurched in new ways to encourage them to take steps of faith toward Christ.

THE RIVER HAS MOVED

The following photo illustrates the shift in American culture from *God consciousness* to having *less of a God consciousness*.

Photo by Sanjeewa Wickramasekera[7]

The bridge in the picture once spanned the Choluteca River, a gift from the nation of Japan to the people of Honduras. Built with steel and concrete, the bridge stood as an engineering marvel which survived the devastating destruction of Hurricane Mitch in 1998 when 150 other bridges were destroyed.

Though built to last, the structure no longer transports people across the river. The bridge is useless.

Why?

The river has moved!

A torrent of rain and flooding redirected the river, causing the water to jump its banks.

Teams of brilliant engineers can do nothing about the present route. No matter how much they wish the river would return to its former course, the channel is set.

The only choice: build a new bridge.

In much the same way, our culture has shifted from its former course. A deluge of media and changing values have redirected the cultural river in America.

Knowing this, the church risks losing its usefulness if we don't revisit the structure. Our church model needs to be reexamined in light of the timeless principles of love-hope-faith which span the widening cultural chasm. We can't expect American values to return to the days where people had more of a God consciousness. As disheartening as it may seem, the culture is moving further and further from God.

Reality today is not the same as the days of our grandparents. The cultural river has moved, and if we want our churches to make an eternal difference, we need to build new bridges of love-hope-faith.

> The cultural river has moved, and if we want our churches to make an eternal difference, we need to build new bridges.

Peggy Noonan, a weekly columnist for *The Wall Street Journal,* believes that "we're in the midst of a rebellion." She cites "the general decline of America's faith in its institutions" and notes that "we feel less respect for almost all of them—the church, the professions, the presidency, the Supreme Court."[8]

As Karl Barth, influential Swiss Protestant theologian from the 20th century, wrote, "Take your Bible and take your newspaper, and read both. But interpret newspapers from your Bible."[9] Increasing our cultural IQ is crucial as Christians. When we take the time to understand the cultural signs, in a small way, we can understand what lies ahead. That's the power of understanding our culture through the lens of God's word.

EVERYDAY MISSIONARIES

I planted four churches that got stranded on dry land before I began to understand the river had moved, and my *bridge* was no longer relevant in helping people far from Christ. If I truly wanted to provide hope for my community, I needed to incorporate what God had revealed to me about love-hope-faith. I needed to engage unchurched people in their own cultural environment and then connect them to Christ and the local church.

I needed to engage unchurched people
in their own cultural environment and
then connect them to Christ and the local church.

I refused to stay marooned on dry land while my surrounding culture moved further and further away from Christ. Violence cut too many lives in the inner city short, many of them children. I needed to act and do so quickly. I needed to join Christ in building the kind of church that reached lost people. Time was short; eternity hung in the balance.

I could no longer expect lost people to come to my church. I needed to go to them. And I knew that would take a shift in our church's scorecard. We would have to create a new culture that redefined what our church considered a success. Darkness only does what darkness knows to do. Sin is ugly, eternally destructive and void of hope. Darkness prevails unless light shows up. If I wanted to light a dark world, I needed to connect with the unchurched around me.

When religious leaders stood ready to stone a woman caught in adultery, Jesus challenged their hypocrisy. If Jesus didn't condemn her; neither should I condemn the lost. He met the woman in the middle of her mess. I needed to do the same. If I could meet my lost neighbors where they were, God could use me to provide hope.

My unchurched neighbors had a difficult time getting involved and understanding unfamiliar biblical concepts. Even my traditions and language left them feeling like outsiders. Because the cultural river had moved, I needed to love my unchurched neighbors in fresh and meaningful ways.

After my first four church plants stagnated, I gathered a small group who also hungered to birth a church focusing on reaching the unchurched.

We intentionally mobilized our congregation to serve the unchurched. Our people became everyday missionaries who learned to follow God's calling to make disciples using their unique gifts. Of course, that all happened outside the walls of the church. Exponential's CEO Todd Wilson says it well: "As leaders, we have to shift our paradigm from *recruiting volunteers to accomplish 'our thing' to mobilizing everyday missionaries in their common and unique callings to accomplish 'God's thing.'"* We need to mobilize God's people God's way—looking at them as more than volunteers but rather, missionaries with a unique calling to carry the fullness of Jesus into the world.

When our church connected with our unbelieving neighbors, we gained social influence for spiritual impact. As a result, we began to see relationships formed where the love of Jesus was extended in powerful ways.

With this small beginning, our new church, Bridge, was born. Making church relevant to the unchurched meant a leadership-directed approach focused on building a great city instead of simply building a great congregation.

> Making church relevant to the unchurched
> meant a leadership-directed approach
> focused on building a great city
> instead of simply building a great congregation.

CHAPTER

3

START WITH LOVE

LOVE-BASED BLOCK PARTIES

When I started hanging out with Diamond and other nonbelieving neighbors, I began to see the block party from their point of view. I tried to reach them based on faith—a faith that was a long way off from where my neighbors were. They didn't know Christian music, and the gospel message I shared seemed out of place for a day focused on fun.

Instead of expecting my neighbors to change, I needed to change. I needed to reach them based on love—a love that inspired hope that could one day lead them to faith in Jesus. I couldn't start from my place of faith. I needed to start with a common ground of love if I wanted to take my neighbors to higher ground.

> I needed to start with a common ground of love
> if I wanted to take my neighbors to higher ground.

Bridge now hosts regular block parties throughout the year that feature Motown and Christian rap and hip-hop music, free food, face painting, a petting zoo, bounce houses and other fun activities for families to enjoy together. The three-legged race and egg toss are both a hit. Smiles and laughter abound. The first block party brought 125 people. Eight summers later, 2,500 children and families attended.

Many attendees are incredulous. "A church is putting on this block party?"

71

I no longer stand on a stage and preach. Instead, a prayer tent is available while a banner references Bridge. I demonstrate love to my unchurched neighbors and have fun getting to know them as friends. Every guest leaves the block party with an invitation to attend Bridge.

Bridge's influence in the community has grown. More and more people come to check out the church that throws fun block parties in the community. Because of our transition to a culture of love-based block parties, Bridge has experienced considerable conversion growth as visitors have surrendered their lives to Christ.

BUILDING A CULTURE OF LOVE IN OUR OUTREACHES

As I considered the complementary principles of love-hope-faith, a picture of how to best *extend* to the unchurched emerged. Thinking beyond the typical Sunday morning and mid-week Bible study meant including love in my approach to reaching people far from Christ. I began to understand the role of building a culture of love in our outreaches, so that our social influence would result in spiritual impact.

Love Outreaches can best be understood as the outreach emphasis of the church to the unchurched. Love outreaches connect believers with unbelievers in authentic relationships focused on encouraging others while having fun together. It is in these neighborhood and citywide activities, like grill-outs and block parties, where love outreaches allow believers to connect with the unchurched. Our discovery was simple, and yet so profound.

When the church serves the community in consistent love outreaches, God works in powerful ways. At Bridge, this includes regular neighborhood clean-up, block parties and other fun service activities where we love and connect with our inner-city neighbors as well as our broader community.

In our modern culture where we can easily isolate ourselves from one another, pastors and church leaders must find cultural inroads that help their congregations engage with the community. These meaningful connections allow us to build trust and establish relationships. For example, acts of service and other community activities are powerful ways to gain social influence for spiritual impact. Our goal is to glorify God by making our faith tangible for people to see. (Matthew 5:16)

Acts of service can include anything from snow removal to home improvement projects while culturally relevant community activities can involve anything from sports to marriage retreats. We want to empower people with hope. These genuine and initial connection points oftentimes open the door for the unchurched to enjoy God's goodness. Ultimately, we want to extend an invitation to church so unbelievers can explore the next step in their faith journey.

Establishing intentional love outreaches is a powerful game changer in reconnecting the church with the unchurched in a nonthreatening way. Starting with love and then creating a pathway for people to visit your church is a great process worth implementing.

LOVING OUR UNBELIEVING NEIGHBORS WHERE WE LIVE

Loving our unbelieving neighbors is the very heart of love-hope-faith. At Bridge, we intentionally focus on three specific areas—loving our neighbors where there's need, where we worship, and where we live. This gives us opportunities to serve together as a church body where there's need and where we worship while also encouraging each other to love our neighbors where we live. When we each make an intentional commitment to love our neighbors in practical ways, the impact is powerful. And if we're mobilizing the people in our church in the way God designed, that impact is two-pronged, on both the unbeliever as well as the people in our congregation God has called us to care for and serve.

Loving our neighbors where we live is just that—loving the community around our home, workplace, and weekly routines. Whether it's the grocery store, shopping mall or fitness center, these are all great places to build relationships, living out what it means to be a witness of Christ's love.

At Bridge, we encourage each other to live out love-hope-faith wherever we go. We developed a strategy of three C's—connect, care, call—to help us be more intentional about loving our neighbors where there's need, where we worship, and where we live. Essentially, we're equipping disciples to make disciples wherever they are and carry the Good News into every crack and cranny.

CONNECT. CARE. CALL.

The practical "love your neighbor" strategy of connect, care and call gives traction to the love-hope-faith revelation. Remembering the letter from the non-Christian neighbor in Chapter 2, we want our approach to be relational, not a cold shoulder approach. We have no ulterior motive other than genuine love and acceptance of our neighbors who are created in the image of God. While we really do want to authentically connect with and care for our neighbors, we also have the hope of calling them into a relationship with Jesus Christ.

> While we really do want to authentically connect with and care for our neighbors, we also have the hope of calling them into a relationship with Jesus Christ.

As leaders wanting to fan this relational approach, we want to establish consistent environments for the members of our congregation to connect with the unchurched in the city. The process is simple. Becoming a good neighbor means intentionally starting with the relationships around us.

Connect is simply building authentic relationships by taking a genuine interest in people. Sharing life stories is an essential component of friendship and a critical building block toward communicating Christ's love.

Many years ago, my wife and I connected with a family who had escaped communist Russia. We listened to their harrowing journey to freedom and their new life in the United States.

Unbeknownst to us, even though they had lived in the States for over seven years, we were the first home to which they'd ever been invited. They shared how rarely an immigrant family connected on a deeper level with Americans. In our conversation, they remarked, "You Americans are very friendly, but you make terrible friends."

Wow.

The power of taking time to connect with and listen to others has meaningful and eternal implications. While we cannot become best friends with everyone, taking a genuine interest in others is valuable and worthwhile. And it is what Jesus has called us to do as disciples.

> The power of taking time to connect with and listen to others has meaningful and eternal implications.

This occurs through listening and learning from others while also finding commonalities. Our connection is driven by our belief that people matter to God, so therefore they matter to us. (Jonah 4:10-11)

Connecting means living with intentionality to engage others around us. This includes relationships at work, in our neighborhoods, through our sports teams and hobbies, even the grocery store—all the people we interact with daily where we live, work and play.

Care takes connecting to a deeper level. When we connect with others, we have a willingness to serve in tangible and practical ways that are meaningful and helpful. Caring for people is simply a gesture of God's love so they might fully know and understand how valuable they are to us and Christ.

> Caring for people is simply a gesture of God's love so they might fully know and understand how valuable they are to us and Christ.

Some examples of caring include: bringing dinner to a sick neighbor, shoveling snow for a busy neighbor, or offering to watch children for a frazzled mom. Examples like these require a Christ-follower to sacrifice time, energy and resources so that Christ's love is expressed in real and authentic ways.

Several years ago, a member at Bridge connected with a gang-affiliated family in the inner city. Despite dangerous conditions and vulgar conversations, this woman never wavered in her positive attitude or care for them. Whether shopping for groceries, transporting children to church activities, visiting those in the hospital or helping with scholarship forms, this woman loved this family on a consistent and powerful basis. Because of her faithful commitment to caring, she has been able to pray for them and share her faith. The family even asked her to conduct a Bible study in their home.

Caring allows us to express Christ's love beyond words. When we demonstrate Christ's love through tangible and practical acts, caring often becomes the very doorway for spiritual impact.

Call is an invitation for people to take the next step in a relationship with Jesus. While calling is the third step in loving your neighbor, sharing something spiritual early on in our relationship prepares the way for spiritual conversations in the future. The longer someone waits to bring up something spiritual, the more difficult it becomes. Sharing something spiritual can be as easy as saying, "I'll pray for you" or "My kids just had a fun event yesterday at our church." The important point is to say something spiritual early on in our connection with others so that talking about spiritual matters appears normal and natural for you.

The key in the calling step is to intentionally help people move forward in their spiritual journey. When Christians are excited about what God is doing in their lives, sharing with others becomes natural. Spiritual conversations and church invitations must occur if unbelievers are to hear and understand the gospel. Most people will open up and talk about their personal spirituality and even visit church if they're asked and treated with dignity.

When we *call* people, our goal is to create as many meaningful opportunities as possible for them to take the next step in their spiritual journey. We truly believe that God is at work in everyday lives, and we want to be available for God to use us. We cannot make people take the next step nor are we trying to pressure those who aren't ready. The Holy Spirit draws people to Christ. Our job is to be passionate about loving others and intentionally creating opportunities for spiritual conversations and invitations.

> The Holy Spirit draws people to Christ.
> Our job is to be passionate about loving others and intentionally creating opportunities for spiritual conversations and invitations.

Joey regularly interacts with his neighbors through grill-outs and shooting hoops with the youth. One of the teens, a Muslim, began to ask Joey questions about his faith. Joey never pressured his neighbor; rather, his lifestyle of love attracts others to Jesus.

Calling does not have to be scary. Sometimes you share the gospel, but often, calling is as simple as inviting someone to church or asking if they need prayer. Calling is the natural outcome of our connection and caring.

We are careful not to be pushy. We want to make sure that our intentional calling is aligned with our connecting and caring for people. Being authentic and genuine is at the heart of loving our neighbors. Connecting, caring and calling must work in harmony with each other. At Bridge, this relational strategy is making significant cultural inroads with the unchurched in our community. As a result, many people have begun a relationship with Christ.

THE BETH SECTION

Beth began attending Bridge at the recommendation of some friends. During a sermon series which challenged our congregation to love their neighbors where they live, Beth took this to heart. She had served in both an area of need and where she worshipped, and now she couldn't wait to love her own neighbors in the suburbs where she lived. She began to celebrate summer family birthdays as neighborhood grill-outs, giving neighbors a reason to hang out together. This turned into a movie night at a local park. Beth told her new friends about her transformation into a passionate follower of Christ and invited them to Bridge.

At last count, Beth was personally responsible for 15 different families attending church on a regular basis. The pastors began to lovingly call the area where she sat *the Beth section*. Beth, Joey and others like them are everyday missionaries who are being disciples that make disciples. Specifically, Beth is a prime example of Exponential's mobilization flywheel I shared about earlier in the Introduction. Her journey as a disciple began at our church, which equipped and mobilized her to become a missionary to her neighborhood and as a result, she has birthed a new gathering of sorts (in our church).

When our congregation takes responsibility for loving the neighbors where they live through the relational strategy of connect, care, call, Bridge has seen incredible growth.

MAKING IT HARD
FOR PEOPLE TO SAY NO TO JESUS

Love is all about connecting with, caring for and calling the unchurched to begin a relationship with Jesus. Our desire is to connect on their terms (not ours) and to care for unbelievers in tangible ways so they see Christ's love working in and through us.

When I led our first team to clean up the neighborhood around my home in the inner city, my instructions brought surprise. "Do not tell anyone about Jesus."

Someone frowned. "But that's not Christian."

I put on my work gloves. "The Bible says we should always be ready to give an answer for the hope that lies within us," I explained myself. "But we don't want to give answers until someone asks us a question."

More volunteers returned the following weekend to mow lawns and pick up trash as a second team worked on renovating a rundown home our church had acquired with help from its partners. We continued to show up and began to invite the neighbors to block parties or grill-outs, never sharing the gospel until someone asked a question.

From those early moments, our attempts to share our faith were no longer a pushy or awkward presentation of the gospel. The natural process of sharing our hearts came when we connected relationally with our neighbors. It didn't take long before people had questions.

Not long after we began the strategy of neighborhood clean-up, a man came outside as we mowed.

"Who are you again?" he asked.

"Bridge Church."

Shock and confusion crossed the man's face. "I didn't know churches did anything."

Wow. What a statement.

Years later, after expanding to serve several more neighborhoods, we approached a woman's house as she got home from work. Before she hurried inside, she turned toward our team. "I know who you guys are. You're Bridge Church. You're the ones who make it hard for people to say no to Jesus."

"You're Bridge Church. You're the ones who make it hard for people to say no to Jesus."

Talk about a major shift. She summed up our hope to be light and salt.

The church becomes powerful when we mobilize missionaries who get out of the seats and into the streets to love our neighbors. The Bible is full of accounts of cities and nations being changed for the better by Christ-followers. (Thessalonica in Acts 17; Ephesus in Acts 19)

Our faith can truly be hope-inspiring to reach people far from Christ when we start with love.

Section I:
DEMONSTRATE LOVE

Key Concept: Consistent love outreaches build passion for the lost and get church members out of the seats and into the streets, maximizing social influence for spiritual impact.

Commitments:

1. Train your congregation in the three C's: connect, care, call.
2. Implement consistent love outreaches.
3. Start serving together once a month.

Questions:

1. How does the faith-hope-love revelation speak to you?

2. What thoughts do you have after reading the letter from your non-Christian neighbor?

3. How would you describe your passion for people far from Christ?

4. How have you seen the river move?

5. What are some ways you can increase your cultural IQ?

6. What would it look like for you to shift your focus from working only with believers and church members, to working with the unchurched?

7. What consistent things have you done to connect your church with the unchurched?

8. How can connect, care and call be implemented in your church?

9. What are some ideas for consistent love outreaches you can implement to build bridges to the unchurched?

10. Would you consider appointing staff and resources intentionally focused on gaining social influence for spiritual impact? Why or why not?

SECTION II:
INSPIRE
HOPE

CHAPTER

4

GOOD WORKS VERSUS GOD'S WORK?

HOPELESSNESS: MY FUTILE ATTEMPTS TO IMPACT THE CITY

Fresh out of prison, Jada and Chandra visited my office with contagious joy. Having participated in a prison ministry that I helped start, they'd faithfully studied the Bible, attended group sessions and completed their prison stay without incident. They made a profession of faith to follow Jesus and committed to our post-prison care program, wanting to reclaim their families for Christ.

The faith-based nonprofit helped with personal needs, such as shelter, clothing and food, but left a void. Not having a church family to replace the bad relationships they'd formed over the years, both women slipped back into their former lifestyle. Within two weeks after leaving prison, Jada died from an overdose and Chandra returned to prison. These women lacked a support system, a new family, and positive role models who could help launch them into a hope-filled future.

Unfortunately, I've seen this cycle repeat time and time again. Without a church family, countless children, youth and families succumb to the negative influences of unhealthy relationships. Many of the same kids in my afterschool programs landed in a casket or a prison cell because of lack of real behavioral change. Countless kids had responded to the gospel and studied the Bible in my programs, yet local and national news articles reported crime, violence, and poverty in the inner city had worsened. These articles, along with frequent visits to funerals and prisons, burdened my heart.

Where was the hope? It seemed so short-lived.

While I realized the vital importance for the church to extend into the city, I didn't know exactly how to proceed beyond the nonprofit and love outreaches. When I first moved into the inner city, the prevailing thought was to work through the faith-based nonprofit—not the church—if you wanted to truly change the world.

The nonprofit sector extended in a way I had not seen in local churches. Whether through homeless shelters, after school programs or other social services, nonprofit organizations meaningfully and practically touched lives. Churches, however, seemed disconnected and distant. They didn't seem to have any activities that impacted the brokenness in my community. With this in mind, I decided to base my transformation strategy on the nonprofit sector.

With renewed passion and an intentional focus to impact my city, I began to engage the unchurched through the faith-based nonprofit, programmatic approach. I wanted my faith to make a difference and change the world.

In my zeal for Christ, I helped start over two dozen faith-based nonprofits to help meet the different needs in the inner city. However, after 15 years of diligent efforts, I realized the incomplete nature of my faith-based nonprofit approach. Children would accept Jesus into their lives and then age out of the program. Without ongoing support, real change diminished, and they lost sight of God. My good works with the nonprofit programmatic approach didn't transform my inner city as I had dreamed and worked toward, nor was there much growth in the church. While I helped to provide needed services and programs, I never saw real cultural change.

UNDERSTANDING BIBLICAL COMPASSION

I worked in the inner city for almost two decades before I understood the reality that my nonprofit-based compassionate outreach efforts did not produce kingdom transformation and disciples. Despite my tireless work and pure motives, my efforts failed. I loved Jesus, but no matter how much energy I exerted, my compassion strategy didn't produce the kind of change I hoped to see. Something was missing.

Compassion, in its most simple definition, is best defined as "concern for the suffering of others." When people see others suffer, compassion moves them to action. Having a desire to alleviate suffering and pain is at the very heart of compassion.

Humans reflect God's image, so people everywhere express some level of compassion and goodness. Even before I became a Christian, a level of compassion and goodness drove me to help others in need through charity.

Unlike human compassion, however, the focus of God's compassion moves people toward salvation and transformation.

> Unlike human compassion, however,
> the focus of God's compassion
> moves people toward salvation and transformation.

As Christians, we are called to advance Christ's kingdom through love and compassion. Our acts of compassion and charity should be a cultural inroad that connects us with others and inspires hope in the good news of the gospel. Our good works and our faith must be intertwined, resulting in the ultimate goal—eternal hope.

Compassionate good works follow a person's faith in Jesus Christ, AND the reversal of this equation means connecting those good works back to faith. Faith and good works, in their pure gospel form, are eternally linked together. (James 2:14-26 NIV) Disjointing faith from good works is simply a humanitarian act of goodness. As Christians, we want to steer clear of the Santa Claus Syndrome—being good for goodness sake. Our compassionate good works must lead somewhere. Christian charity must move people to Christ and his church—God's answer for a broken world, his hope for lost people.

WHAT IS ULTIMATE SUFFERING?

If the heart of compassion is a heart to alleviate suffering, then Christians must understand the depth of real suffering. Ultimate suffering, according to God's word, is life without Jesus—to live without eternal hope. (Luke 16; Romans 6:23) To the world, this is a radical way to view suffering.

> Ultimate suffering, according to God's word, is life without Jesus—to live without eternal hope.

Christianity is counter-intuitive. If we want to be the *greatest*, God's word says we should become the *least*. If we want to be *first*, we should be *last*. If we really want to *live*, we must *die*. These counter-intuitive statements reveal the vast differences between the natural mind and the mind of God as described in Romans 8:7. In fact, the human mind is often at odds against God's thinking.

Because God's ways are not man's ways, compassion is seen differently from the world's view. Christian compassion reexamines suffering beyond only the natural—physical, mental or emotional needs. Christians desire to alleviate suffering at the deepest level of pain—spiritual. They view suffering through the lens of an eternal perspective.

> Christians view suffering through the lens of an eternal perspective.

For example, poverty is more than physical. Providing a pathway to employment and economic gain is good but does nothing for the poverty of the soul. We can fix up every house in the inner city, but if there isn't a heart change for the occupants, the new houses will ultimately deteriorate. The heart and soul are bankrupt without the richness of Jesus at the center of life. As written in Mark 8:36, "What good is it for someone to gain the whole world, yet forfeit their soul?" (NIV)

When caring for the sick, a Christ-follower goes beyond focusing on the physical need to addressing the pain that occurs in life without Jesus as healer.

Broken relationships create sorrow and loneliness, exposing the basic human need to be fully loved. Christians point to the most intimate relationship available—with Jesus.

Christian compassion reexamines suffering and addresses both the natural and the spiritual. We know that no matter how much suffering we alleviate on earth, eternity is in the balance. If ultimate suffering is life without Jesus, then Christian compassion must be inclusive of both the temporary and the eternal. (Acts 19; Jeremiah 22:16; Jeremiah 29:7)

Ultimate hope is eternal hope.

> If ultimate suffering is life without Jesus,
> then Christian compassion must be inclusive
> of both the temporary and the eternal.

THE SHALLOWNESS OF HUMANITARIAN GOODNESS

In twenty years, I helped start over two dozen nonprofit organizations committed to supporting and developing inner city youth and their families. Whether it was an after-school or prison program, faith-filled, young charismatic leaders led these nonprofits with a passion to see lives transformed by the good news of Jesus.

Well over a thousand youth and families participated in the programs. These kids and their families genuinely loved participating in our programs, and the leaders genuinely loved working with them. However, in twenty years, there's been little to no evidence of increased spiritual transformation, discipleship or church growth. Many of the youth continue to engage in destructive behaviors while the overall climate of the inner city continues to struggle with crime, violence, school dropouts and high unemployment.

A Christian tract I once read told me to give my life to Christ, read my Bible, pray, go to church, and do good. The words *do good* struck me. When did American Christianity reduce our mission to *doing good* and *being nice*? Early Christians included church at the center of all their activities and made incredible sacrifices, including becoming martyrs, to reach and disciple those far from Christ.

Overwhelmed with the disheartening results, my leaders and I wrestled with several questions.

- What is the difference when a Christian does something compared to a non-Christian doing the same thing? In other words, if Christianity is so radically different from the world's way of doing something, what are the unique differences?

- What does it mean for a Christian to show Christ's love? Do we simply express *goodness*, or is there something entirely different when we express *God's love*?

- Are we displaying the *kingdom of God*, or are we displaying an *earthly good*? Do we offer *temporary benefits* or *eternal hope*?

Sadly, twenty years later, many of the youth we've worked with are dead, in prison or living an unhealthy, destructive lifestyle. Seeing the lack of transformation has weighed heavy on my heart over the years. These disheartening realities prompted me to dig deeper in understanding what was missing.

FROM TEMPORARY HELP
TO ETERNAL HOPE

Viktor Frankl, a world-renowned physicist who survived Auschwitz during World War II, said you could predict who would die in the concentration camp. It wasn't the sickest or the weakest, but the person who had given up hope. When you give up hope, you lose the will to survive.[10]

So, if hope is such a powerful thing, where do we find hope?

There's a profound difference in *good works* alone which bring blessings from God and *God's work* which brings a relationship with God. Is our hope based on the blessings or on a relationship?

Good works bring temporary results. God's work leads people to repentance and eternal hope. The church should do both. God's work always includes good works, but good works alone don't necessarily include God's work. God's work involves an invitation to a heart change and real transformation. In our humanity, we can all do good things, but that is different from God's work which leads to eternal hope and salvation.

> God's work always includes good works, but good works alone don't necessarily include God's work.

The Bible pairs good works with kingdom building. Paul writes in Colossians 3:17, "Let every detail in your lives—words, *actions*, whatever—be done in the name of the Master, Jesus, thanking God the Father every step of the way." (MSG) Likewise, John 10:25 says, "The *works* that I do in my Father's name, *they bear witness* of me." (NKJV) Matthew 5:16 further reiterates this concept. "Let your light so shine before men, that they may *see* your *good works*, and *glorify your Father* in heaven." (NKJV)

Could a non-Christian group do the same thing the church is doing? If so, how is our good work related to God's work? For example, if the church is running a food pantry, how is that any different than a food pantry run by a secular organization? Wouldn't it be better to build relationships with those coming to the food pantry with the ultimate goal of connecting them to the church, a lifelong family?

Bottom line—needs don't create a relationship; needs create dependency. The goal is to *meet people*, not simply *meet needs*. We can meet needs once a relationship begins. If the church is not connected to the good work, then we offer momentary relief rather than offering a womb to tomb support system.

> The goal is to *meet people*, not simply *meet needs*.

I love the passage in Romans 2:4 which describes how "the goodness of God leads to repentance." (NKJV) In other words, the good work of God takes people somewhere. God's work doesn't simply stop at a temporary benefit. God's work leads people to Christ and the fullness He offers.

> God's work leads people to Christ
> and the fullness He offers.

SHOWING & SHARING THE GOSPEL

We live in a broken, messy and challenging world. More than ever, God's grace and truth is needed. Brokenness is seen in the sick and hurting, in the exploitation of people, in hunger and homelessness and in many harmful and hurtful realities of this world. The overarching question begs us to ask: How should pastors, church leaders and Christians respond?

Many faith-based organizations in America focus on helping and improving communities. While I believe the intentions are sincere and that the work provides significant *temporary good*, most of these nonprofit organizations are not directly connected with a church, so they do not experience much discipleship fruit or lasting change.

Tyrell didn't have much opportunity. As the son of a pimp and a drug abuser, his early life was hard. He grew up in a low-income housing project across the street from a faith-based nonprofit. He not only enjoyed the activities of the faith-based nonprofit, he enjoyed playing basketball with another nonprofit in the community.

While many of these programs helped Tyrell navigate his childhood, these programs fell short as he entered adolescence. Most of his cousins belonged to gangs, so Tyrell found acceptance and love by joining.

Programmatic nonprofits do not have a support system from the womb to the tomb. Tyrell aged out of the programs and slipped through the cracks as he got older and eventually ended up in prison for selling drugs. While his first prison sentence was short-lived, he quickly returned for armed robbery and attempted murder.

While in prison he surrendered his life to Jesus and began attending church services. When he left prison on parole, he found a new church family who filled the gap left by his old gang. Tyrell graduated from college with a Bible degree and is a pastor today.

Tyrell is a great example of the importance of being connected to a local church. I made a radical shift in my nonprofit approach as I discovered God's work places the church at the center and focus of all our good activities.

> God's work places the church
> at the center and focus of all our good activities.

Conversion growth is a biblical priority along with improving the community. Community improvement has temporary value if the church isn't central. Showing and sharing the gospel, with a focus on getting people connected to the church, is essential. If the church isn't a direct part of the overall equation, conversions to Christ and discipleship doesn't happen at the power and rate that it should. Improving our community is important, but not at the expense of losing our primary mission. In our attempt to do good work, we must not lose sight of sharing the gospel to a broken world.

The apostle Paul defines what it truly means to follow Jesus and live for him. He makes it very clear that our mission in life is to glorify God by testifying to the gospel of the grace of God. "But my life is worth nothing to me unless I use it for finishing the work assigned me by the Lord Jesus—the work of telling others the Good News about the wonderful grace of God." (Acts 20:24 NKJV)

In living for Christ in a broken world, everything a disciple maker does points to the grace of God. We *demonstrate good works* and *communicate good news*. It's not one or the other; it is both. Building a bridge between our *good deeds* and our *good news* is essential in accomplishing God's work.

Two Types of Compassion	
GOD'S WORK	**GOOD WORKS**
Eternal Kingdom	Temporary Humanitarian

Bridge began to demonstrate good works through consistent love outreaches, but communicating the good news came with new challenges. As people began to show up at church because of the outreaches, the gaps became noticeable. Our church culture at Bridge was unfamiliar to the unchurched, so we struggled with getting guests to return. How could we communicate the good news and bring eternal hope to our neighbors without widening the chasm?

The answer came in the love-hope-faith revelation. Hope was the key to bridge the gap between our love outreaches and seeing people accept Christ by faith. We needed to build a culture of hope in the church if we wanted to reach the unchurched, so Bridge began to intentionally elevate and inspire hope.

Chapter

5

ELEVATING
A CULTURE OF HOPE

BUILDING A BRIDGE OF HOPE

As a teenager, James found excitement in alcohol, drugs, and a life of crime in the inner city. As his life spiraled out of control, he knew that he needed to go to church, but was hurt when the pastoral leadership changed.

James lived a few houses down from members at Bridge. This family intentionally hosted block parties and hung out with the kids on the block. When they invited James and his wife to church, James agreed, knowing his own life lacked a deeper connection to God and people.

Shocked, James couldn't believe what he found at Bridge. Instead of a weekly fashion show he'd known at church, joy lined the faces of the greeters he encountered. He couldn't believe how many people were genuinely glad to see him. Before James even got to his seat, he felt like family with all the high fives and hugs he received. James couldn't wait to invite his wife to experience this *different church* where people got excited you came. His only warning to her: they like to hug a lot.

Not only did James's wife join him the following week, the couple now attends Bridge every week where they are leaders committed to making other new people feel just as welcomed.

Would a nonbelieving guest at your church feel like an outsider? Do guests need a translator to understand the jargon? Do we strive to develop a welcoming culture where genuine relationships form, and visitors feel like part of the family?

Christians are called to be peacemakers and bridge-builders, reconciling a broken, confused and lost world to Christ. If we're not careful, we often take one of two approaches to our surrounding culture. We can either get caught up in the flow of all that's happening around us and become pro-cultural, pursuing the American dream, or we can become anti-cultural, angry, bitter and protesting the evils of society.

Neither approach mirrors God's heart and God's hope for a broken world.

Christians should become **counter-cultural**. We are *in* this world, but not *of* this world, so we promote God's kingdom culture instead of conforming to popular culture or becoming bitter about the ills of society. Rather than *assimilate*, we *infiltrate* the culture with the good news of Jesus. When we love people, they see we have something significantly more powerful than their current reality. (John 18:36; 1 Peter 2:11-12)

If Christians are going to make an eternal difference, we must build a positive, joy-filled kingdom culture. Rather than concentrate on our personal preferences, we must use our gifts and unique calling to identify with the unchurched in our community.

Why don't more people walk through the doors of our churches?

Many unchurched people describe church as boring and churched people as unfriendly and cliquish. They often feel judged and unwelcomed. Thom Rainer, in his blog *Growing Healthy Churches Together*, refers to this cliquish mentality as the *Holy Huddle Syndrome*. "Church members naturally gravitate to people they know when they go to a worship service. They already have relational connections. The members thus perceive they are friendly because they are friendly to each other. Unfortunately, guests are not included."[11]

If we want to partner with Christ in building a church that reaches the lost, we need to take hospitality to a whole new level. Identify leaders who have the gift of hospitality and encouragement, then train them to be hope agents who up the friendly factor. Intentionally focus on engagement with visitors. Only then can we begin to build a bridge of hope between our church culture and the culture of the unchurched.

FIRST IMPRESSIONS

Elevating hope in our church services is a powerful way to assimilate the lost into our church culture. Our outreaches can be effective, but if we forget to elevate and inspire hope on a Sunday morning, the lost will struggle to connect.

How can we help the unchurched come to faith in Christ? Is the jump from a love outreach to attending Sunday morning services too much if we aren't intentional about elevating hope?

First impressions are huge. When guests walk into a church, the first few minutes dramatically influence their return rate. Churches must be welcoming, or we risk losing an opportunity to impact the unchurched with the love of Christ. Building a culture of hope is critical to serving the unchurched. It has become one of the metrics on our scorecard that tells us how we're doing. Without hope—the connection between love and faith—the unchurched won't take the next spiritual step.

Elaine Storkey, president of Tearfund, a leading Christian relief and development charity, observed that a lot of people would be unsure what to expect if they did visit church. "The church, for a lot of people, is a very strange place these days. They're not familiar with what's going on inside the building, with the form of service, with the way people gather, with what they say, how they pray." She went on to explain that pastors and church leaders have "got to wake up to the reality that there is this big cultural gap between churched and non-churched."[12]

"The church, for a lot of people, is a very strange place these days. They're not familiar with what's going on inside the building, with the form of service, with the way people gather, with what they say, how they pray."

LIVING A "JOY-NORMOUS" LIFESTYLE

Fear is the number one emotion non-Christians experience when they visit a church for the first time.[13] Visitors are usually anxious and uncomfortable because they don't know what to expect. *What will people think? Where do I go? What are they going to do? What will they expect of me?*

Creating an atmosphere of hope and joy helps alleviate fear. People want to be happy. As Christians, we have more than happiness; we have joy that fills us, despite our circumstances. To engage with the unchurched, we need to make sure that our countenance and church services don't appear sullen, somber or even unfriendly to visitors. We need to be mindful of our nonverbal communication. Even if we're having a bad day, we need to reflect our joy. If we would simply *look happy*, unchurched people would take notice and be drawn to us.

Walls go up when people are afraid. No matter how good the sermon, visitors won't hear what is said if they feel uncomfortable. Oftentimes people don't remember what is said. They do, however, remember how they felt. With this in mind, we must help guests feel at ease and welcomed. Today, more than ever, the unchurched are looking for a friendly culture of hope and joy that will facilitate their pursuit of Christ.

ELEVATING HOPE

Imbedded traditions cannot dictate how we live and move forward in our future. It's easy to get stuck in our routines and rituals, accepting the comfortable rather than choosing to be stretched. Church leaders must intentionally commit to changing their scorecard, both personally and for their church, and develop a meaningful and relevant culture that engages with the unchurched—while always maintaining the integrity of the gospel.

We build a culture of hope when we intentionally elevate the following:

- **Attitude.** Outward expressions of joy are uplifting, contagious and hopeful.

- **Activities.** Meaningful and engaging activities impact both the churched and unchurched.

- **Language**. As Christ-followers, our language must communicate encouragement, value and hope.

- **Atmosphere & Environment.** When people walk into our churches, we want them to encounter the dynamic and powerful presence of Jesus.

Everything from the parking lot and greeting team to music and preaching must be examined through the eyes of a first-time guest. Choose to elevate energy and enthusiasm, and watch—a culture of hope will build.

THE CULTURAL VALUE OF ENERGY AND ENTHUSIASM

People love to have fun. Being happy and having fun is attractive to others. If the *joy of the Lord* is truly our strength, then joy is powerful when we express it to others. (Nehemiah 8:10 NIV) Joy and hope are contagious.

> If the *joy of the Lord* is truly our strength, then joy is powerful when we express it to others.

Our staff and volunteers make up several dynamic teams, including the wave team, the parking lot team, the usher team, and the music team. These volunteers are trained to consider themselves as the *first impressions* team and encouraged to have lots of fun as they welcome and serve people who are arriving. Every team member is a carrier of this hope-filled culture; each is critical in setting the tone, atmosphere and climate of the church service.

At Bridge, we start with celebration. Our pre-service party begins in the parking lot. A DJ plays up-beat music while kids are often found shooting hoops or tossing around a football—even building snowmen during the winter months. Many times, people driving by Bridge stop out of curiosity because our wave team stands along the main street waving and smiling to those driving by the church. We've even had an individual stop his car, roll down his window and hand us a donation because our expressions of joy and kindness encouraged him. When it rains, we have our teams in the parking lot with umbrellas. People are strategically placed in and around our campus to greet guests and make people feel a sense of hope and excitement.

Team members practice the **six "H's." High fives**, **handshakes**, **heartfelt conversations**, and **side hugs** are part of our regular routine as we greet visitors. We are positioned to lend a **helping hand** whenever needed and always **handoff** guests by introducing them to others, so they continue to feel connected.

The **three-minute rule** is also a powerful way to engage visitors. For three minutes before and after the church service, our team cannot talk to anyone they know. They must find guests and be available to help in any way possible. This rule has become such a part of our church culture, the time has naturally expanded, so we now lovingly call it the "thirty-minute rule."

Deena, a member of Bridge, resisted the idea of engaging others. "That's not me," she confided, so I challenged her to see this as an opportunity to impact someone's life for Christ. A decade later, Deena not only engages guests regularly at Bridge, she disciples unchurched young women. She never would have done this without being stretched to engage others on Sunday mornings.

She has found her sweet spot as she follows the call to make disciples. Remember God looks at people as more than volunteers. He created each of us to carry his fullness into the world. To authentically connect with others and do it repeatedly, our people, like Deena, need to be in their sweet spot—and not simply filling an empty slot.

Elevating hope through authentic energy and uncontrived enthusiasm opens doors for the unchurched to encounter Christ. A sense of excitement and enthusiasm is powerful as people connect at church for the first time. When people sense something is happening at church, they are more likely to connect. They see our hope is worth pursuing.

> When people sense something is happening at church, they are more likely to connect.

Many pastors are intrigued by the love-hope-faith revelation when they hear me speak at conferences. Curious, they fly to Omaha to experience the energy at our love outreaches and hope-filled Sunday morning services. Pastors leave inspired to implement the same principles of love-hope-faith into their churches back home.

Creating a culture of hope is an important game changer in the church that is committed to reaching people far from Christ.

Chapter

6

IMPLEMENTING
A CULTURE OF HOPE

BUILDING AN EARLY ADOPTER TEAM

Changing the prevailing church culture to one that elevates and inspires hope can be difficult. At Bridge we started small. To begin elevating hope on Sunday mornings, we built an early adopter team.

I took our team through a series of challenging questions regarding our ability to reach nonbelievers. Sadly, we were not influencing unbelievers at the level we desired.

"How many times have we shared our faith and led someone to Christ in the last year?" I asked my team of twelve leaders.

Combined, we remembered three occasions over an entire year.

Yikes!

Our core team considered ourselves mission-driven, and yet, nothing was further from the truth. We simply did not live with a sense of urgency as Ephesians 5:16 describes. We had somehow ignored what our hearts knew Christ wanted for our lives. Instead of joining God in His invitation to witness to unbelievers (Acts 1:8), we had been busy working only with believers. We did a lot of ministry activity, but we missed God's heart for *lost people*.

I asked our team to participate in a simple exercise.

- If God wants to rescue and save people, does he want to use you? If so, then write down how many people you think God wants you to impact this week in your circle of influence—people you connect with through your neighborhood, work, school, hobbies, social group, family network, etc.

Between the 12 of us, we came up with nearly 50 people. Our spiritual concern for others elevated, we left the meeting expecting God to show up. The following week we shared so many stories, our meeting went for hours.

I shared how I sensed God leading me to Aisle 4 at the grocery store when I asked him to show me who to encourage. A woman started to cry when I told her I didn't know the challenges she faced, but felt God wanted her to know everything would be all right. She explained how her husband had left her, and she had no clue what to do. We prayed, and she left with a newfound assurance that God cared for her.

Others shared stories of how they invited people to church while others talked to neighbors they had never met. This same group who could only remember sharing their faith three times the entire previous year came back with nearly four dozen stories of how God used them just over the previous week.

Our antennas went up; we discovered how God worked all around us and how he wanted to use us. Not only did each of us get excited about how God used us as individuals, hearing the stories of others increased our faith.

As you build your early adopter team, repeat this activity for several weeks until this becomes an integral part of the culture of your leaders, and they begin to see themselves as everyday missionaries "sent" to carry the fullness of Jesus to our unique circles of influence. To keep the vision at the forefront of your team, revisit the exercise at least monthly.

We can't expect our congregation to change without leaders who see the need to change their scorecard, cast a vision to multiply disciples and then model how to be agents of hope to the lost. Building an early adopter team is essential to forming leaders who act as thermostats, not thermometers. We want to cultivate hero makers who intentionally *set* the climate and atmosphere in our church rather than simply accept the temperature and follow imbedded cultural traditions.

As your team follows the call to make disciples and is used powerfully by Christ, celebrate these God-sized stories with your congregation. When communicated from the pulpit, a vision is cast. Momentum will begin to build as personal stories are shared, and we engage in consistent love outreaches as a church. People will begin to catch the vision: God is up to something, and he wants the entire church to be part of multiplying disciples.

THE CULTURAL VALUE
OF EXPECTATION

Apathy had always been an issue in my earlier church plants. Many people showed up to church on Sunday but never really got engaged. I wanted every person in my congregation to arrive with an expectation that God would show up and do something powerful. Changing the mindset, attitudes and actions of my congregation wasn't easy, but well worth the effort.

The early adopter team members became the catalyst— the essential ingredient—toward cultivating a hope-filled culture. Training the early adopter team to be sensitive to the unchurched and to see themselves as everyday missionaries who are critical to the success of seeing unbelievers enjoy service and then return.

When Sunday morning is more than going through the motions, the church family comes together and experiences the power and presence of God. My leadership team needs to set an expectation that Jesus is going to show up, meet us right where we are, and take us higher. Our staff and volunteers make a commitment to gather one hour before Sunday service for pre-service TIP time: **training**, **inspiration** and **prayer**.

<u>TIP</u> Time

- **T**raining our team with appropriate hope-filled language, social interaction, hospitality, and

128

greeting skills builds a powerful culture that connects with, values and relates with unchurched and churched visitors. TIP time is only 10-15 minutes in length before leaders position themselves to greet guests. This training time powerfully reinforces the culture we are building at Bridge.

- **I**nspiration fills us with a powerful level of expectation and excitement for what God is going to do during our time together. Our leadership shares inspiring stories, scripture and encouragement to elevate our team with expectations of what Christ will do in the service.

- **P**rayer binds us together and centers everything we do in Christ and His plan for our service. The power of prayer, combined with our obedience to live-out a hope-filled culture while serving others, is a winning combination to impact a lost and broken world.

During TIP time, we set the tone in building a hope-filled atmosphere. We communicate expectations that the day will be filled with God's wonder and presence as we become the hands and feet of Jesus to guests who attend our Sunday morning service.

FAITH IT 'TIL YOU FEEL IT

Life has many ups and downs. People don't feel hope-filled every day. So how do leaders inspire hope on Sunday mornings when they're having a bad day?

At Bridge, we adopted a motto: "Faith it 'til you feel it." Knowing that we may not always feel upbeat, we have faith that God is going to show up. Because of this, we faith our attitude and actions until we feel hope. As Christians, we choose to see the glass as half full and getting fuller. Training our leaders to "faith it 'til you feel it" is critical if we want to create a culture of hope. We don't fake it; we faith it. (Hebrews 11:1)

When members of Bridge admit that our hope-filled culture doesn't always feel natural, our response is one of expectation. If we can get excited over sporting events, why can't we get excited about what God is doing through our local church? As leaders, we don't have the luxury of following. People look to us to set the tone and temperature of the church.

Does that mean we can't have bad days? No. We realize that serving is not about us—it's about others. While we do not deny the reality of what we're facing, we do, in Jesus' name, deny the finality of our circumstances. "We fix our eyes not on what is seen, but on what is unseen, since what is seen is temporary, but what is unseen is eternal." (2 Corinthians 4:18 NIV) When we're focused on the eternal, we can soar on wings like eagles. (Isaiah 40:31) Our hope allows us to rise above life's storms. When we radiate joy, our hope becomes contagious. This sets the tone of our culture.

MUSIC AND PREACHING

Understanding how to best utilize music is critical when engaging unbelievers. *If our focus includes unbelievers, what role should music play? Can we expect non-Christians to worship the same as Christians?*

Music was a point of discussion with my worship director when Bridge first started. As I flipped through the pages of the worship book he'd used for years, song after song had a similar emphasis in reflection and adoration. After almost an hour of discussion, only 6 of the 309 songs seemed best suited to relate to an unchurched person.

Introspective music helps believers express their adoration but lacks meaning for unbelievers. While people have different tastes, congregations focused on the unchurched understand the power of celebratory, up-beat music. While this shift might seem minimal, music plays a big role in creating a culture of hope for the unchurched.

Like music, communicating the good news of Jesus begins with our audience, not us. Our culture today prefers interactive and experience-oriented learning. People want to hear about relevant issues, so communicators need to avoid church jargon and explain scriptural references with familiar language.

Joy and humor also play a powerful role as we relate with unbelievers in ways that are authentic, genuine and disarming. In a stressed-out society, light-hearted and funny communicators bring hope and enjoyment while engaging people in ways that are insightful and helpful.

Music and preaching can make or break the experience for a first-time guest. Churches that focus on reaching unbelievers are sensitive to the powerful roles that music and preaching play.

CELEBRATING LIFE-CHANGE

The Bible makes it very clear that we are all sinners in need of a savior. (Romans 3:23) We were all once lost before Jesus found us (Luke 15:24) and blind before Jesus gave us sight. (John 9:25) Like the apostle Paul, every Christ-follower experiences a Damascus Road conversion where God radically turns our world upside down and leads us into a radical life change. (Romans 2:4 MSG)

I have some friends who met Jesus in prison. When they surrendered to Jesus, they repented of their criminal life choices and began a new life in Christ. My conversion story, however, looked different. I thought growing up in church meant I was a Christian. Until college, I didn't understand my faith was actually the faith of my parents. I considered myself a good person when I compared myself to others. Until I recognized my brokenness and sinful nature, I didn't know the depth of my own depravity. Jesus was *important* to my life, but radical change happened when he became the **center** of my life. I shifted from building my life around my plans to building my life around his plans. I began to focus on building his kingdom versus building my own empire.

When people have a conversion experience, they surrender control and let Jesus direct their everyday lives. No longer the boss, they're under new management. Sharing conversion stories with the entire congregation is a powerful reminder that God still transforms lives.

I like the BE-DO-GO framework that Exponential has developed: Every Christian is called to (BE) a disciple, who makes disciples (DO) wherever they GO! He not only transforms us; He wants to use our story to encourage transformation in others.

Telling current faith stories and sharing how God has used us (BE-DO-GO) inspires and elevates growth in our congregation to reach others for Christ. When congregation members regularly share how they prayed with a waitress or encouraged someone at the gym or invited a neighbor to church, everyone is inspired to step up their game and be mobilized for Christ's vision and mission. Celebrating these ongoing faith stories and being intentional about how we mobilize God's people act as a catalyst to produce growth in the congregation and help us relate and empathize with those who are without hope.

> Telling current faith stories inspire and elevate growth in our congregation to reach others for Christ.

Having regular baptisms is equally important. Baptisms are a public declaration of the inward transformation of Christ's power in our lives. When conversions are celebrated regularly through baptism, the congregation is reminded that lost people are God's priority. Baptisms testify to God's transforming work in our personal lives, reacquainting us with the incredible love, joy and peace we received when Jesus forgave our sins and set us free.

Leaders fan the flame of passion for lost people in our congregations by sharing conversion and ongoing faith stories. When people are continually processing and practicing these stories, they live with a level of hope that overflows in conversation and relationships with others.

As we roll up our sleeves together as a congregation, commit to telling conversion and ongoing faith stories on a regular basis. Brag on God. What you celebrate and elevate, you reproduce.

> What you celebrate and elevate, you reproduce.

FOLLOW-UP

It takes 28 days to create a new habit. While church attendance may be familiar and normal for church members, the unchurched are undertaking a completely new venture when they walk into a church. No matter how much they enjoyed a service, getting out of bed on Sunday mornings can be a challenge as they are creating new habits in their life.

Follow-up is extremely critical to nonbelievers returning to church. When guests feel encouraged after a service, a positive follow-up experience within 24 hours shows they are valued. At Bridge, every guest receives a phone call follow-up. These phone calls consist of a relaxed conversation about their week, their thoughts about the service, and an invitation to return the following Sunday.

Follow-up has proven critical in helping nonbelievers create new faith habits. There is a direct correlation between unbelievers coming back to church and their potential for a life-changing relationship with Jesus and His church family.

People are looking for happiness, meaningful relationships and purpose. To address the search for happiness, we intentionally create a Sunday morning celebration where people can be inspired, uplifted and experience the joy of the Lord. Small groups focus on the need for meaningful relationships by connecting people in a more intimate family environment where depth of relationship is built. Finally, our consistent serving opportunities act as a catalyst in helping people see themselves as everyday missionaries and develop a sense of purpose through giving of themselves to benefit the larger community.

Research shows that getting people involved within the first six months is key to retention.[14] Whether new attendees serve during an outreach event or on Sunday morning, they are more likely to stay connected with the church. But again, don't just plug them into a slot. Commit to helping people discover and live out their primary and unique callings. This consistent interaction dramatically helps unchurched people discover their sweet spot and become Christ-followers and members in a church family.

SENSITIVITY VERSUS COMPROMISE

Lives are messy. Guests who haven't experienced church may not meet our expectations of behavior in a typical church setting. As they wrestle with new ideas and beliefs, the unchurched may say things that contradict our Christian beliefs.

So how do we extend grace to the unchurched and give them time to form healthy relationships and authentically consider the claims of Christ?

People can *belong* to Bridge before they ever *believe*.

Jude 1:22-23 says, "Go easy on those who hesitate in the faith. Go after those who take the wrong way. Be tender with sinners, but not soft on sin." (MSG) What would it look like to go *easy on* and *go after* unbelievers who took the wrong way? Being sensitive to the unchurched doesn't mean compromising our beliefs. Rather, to engage the unchurched, we must rethink our approach to those disconnected from church. We can't change unbelievers, but we can love people and let the Holy Spirit work on their hearts.

> Being sensitive to the unchurched
> doesn't mean compromising our beliefs.

As Christians, we can't react in shock or judgment. Arguing won't move unbelievers to change. Our job is to love. When differences arise, we give space and grace to allow the Holy Spirit to do the convicting and changing. Jacob wrestled with God before he had a change of heart. Likewise, unbelievers need time to wrestle with God and the truth of scripture before their behavior and beliefs align with his heart.

Jesus showed sensitivity and kindness to unbelievers. Shouldn't we do the same?

137

SUNDAY MORNING CELEBRATION

When non-Christians come to church, they want to sense the energy, authenticity and vibrancy of our love for Jesus. They want to know that what we offer is worth pursuing.

> When non-Christians come to church, they want to sense the energy, authenticity and vibrancy of our love for Jesus. They want to know that what we offer is worth pursuing.

The Reveal Study, a survey of over 1,000 churches conducted by the Willow Creek Association, concluded that Sunday morning church service is best suited for those exploring Christ and early believers growing in Christ.[15] Even Paul recognized his need to start with the basics to reach his worldly audience. (1 Corinthians 3:2) While mature believers need solid food, early believers thrive on milk. (1 Peter 2:2)

At Bridge, our transition to a Sunday morning hope-filled culture of celebration, hospitality and joy powerfully connects us to unbelievers. We don't water down the gospel, but we present more solid food in small groups and specific discipleship classes.

By implementing a culture of hope, a friendly, more welcoming church is better prepared to attract conversion growth. Hope-inspiring churches celebrate God's goodness and powerfully engage with the lost—

opening a doorway for unbelievers to embrace faith. Creating a culture of hope is possibly the most profound way churches can connect with the unchurched on a Sunday morning.

Section II:
INSPIRE HOPE

Key Concept: When unchurched people show up on Sunday morning, we need to be ready to receive them. Adding a few simple, guest-friendly strategies can elevate and inspire hope on a Sunday morning.

Commitments:

1. Up the friendly factor with the 6 H's: high fives, handshakes, heartfelt conversations, side hugs, lending a helping hand and handing off guests by introducing them to others.
2. Build an early adopter team, challenging them to see themselves as everyday missionaries who regularly reach out to the unchurched.
3. Implement TIP time and create a culture of energy, enthusiasm and expectation.
4. Regularly share conversion and ongoing faith stories.
5. Celebrate regular baptisms.
6. Be sensitive to the unchurched in the selection of worship music and language used in preaching.

Questions:

1. Why is it important to distinguish between the two types of compassion?

2. Evaluate your current outreach strategy. Do you need to be more intentional in making good works God's work?

3. What is the number one emotion non-Christians experience when they visit a church for the first time?

4. How can your church be more happy, friendly and welcoming to guests?

5. What strategies can you adopt to build a culture of hope and expectation?

6. How does the church change its scorecard and become a thermostat setting the temperature and affecting the culture rather than a thermometer only reflecting the temperature?

7. How can we celebrate conversion and ongoing faith stories as a congregation?

8. How can we increase retention after guests visit?

SECTION III:
UNLEASH
FAITH

.

FAITH-SHAPING DISRUPTIONS

A FALSE ASSUMPTION

One morning I met a young boy of about six years old heading to school. When I wished him a good morning, he muttered a string of vulgar words and then said, "What's so good about it?"

My heart sank. I couldn't help but wonder what had shaped someone so young to be so angry. If unchecked, the boy's anger would lead to a future in jail or death. The brokenness in this young boy broke my heart, and God used it to show me the heart of discipleship.

For years, as I worked to develop the faith of my congregation, I assumed that giving people the right information would cause them to believe the right things, and in turn, translate to faith and right behavior. I spent years pouring over the scriptures, preaching, teaching and leading countless Bible studies. The king of information, I was informed and bent on informing others. Focused on developing a personal relationship with God, I thought discipleship meant more worship, deeper prayer and increased Bible knowledge. I completely missed helping our congregation develop a purposeful relationship with God where we loved people far from Christ and shared our faith as we became disciples who were mobilized to make disciples.

The longer I lived in the inner city and the more I experienced the tragedy around me, the more I began to think differently about discipleship. Until I began to interact with my neighbors, I didn't understand how the

149

daily struggles with fatherlessness, abuse and poverty had formed my neighbors.

MORE FORMED THAN INFORMED

Anthropologists say that our behavior is directly affected by what we value, and those values are influenced by our beliefs. Our beliefs, however, are not *informed* as I had previously thought. Rather, our beliefs come from our worldview which has been predominantly *formed* by years of experiences. In other words, we are more *formed* than *informed*. Even as Christians, God's word doesn't shape us until we become doers, not just hearers. As James 1:22 says, "Do not merely listen to the word, and so deceive yourselves. Do what it says." (NIV)

We are more *formed* than *informed*.

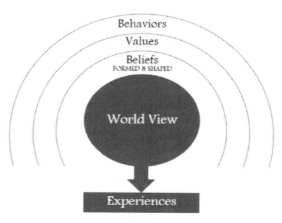

My son-in-law and oldest daughter are missionaries in Thailand. One day in the thick of Chiang Mai traffic, Ben rushed to help a young man who'd been thrown from his motorcycle. A crowd had gathered, but no one helped. Ben ripped his shirt to use as a tourniquet and yelled for someone to call an ambulance. Again, no one moved. Frustrated, Ben had to make the call himself.

Because Thailand is a Buddhist country, people believe in good and bad karma. According to their beliefs, bad things happen because people with bad karma deserve punishment. Buddhist people don't want bad karma to transfer to them, so no one would get close to the young man and help. Even though Ben *informed* them of the need to help, their Buddhist beliefs *formed* by their daily experiences in a culture which reinforced these values, dictated their behavior.

THE POWER OF EXPERIENCES

As a pastor with a heart to unleash people to become the kind of disciples who live out their calling in practical and powerful ways, this was a huge revelation to me. Our worldview is primarily influenced by our experiences. We can't expect our congregations to be formed into powerful disciples unless we give them *faith-shaping* opportunities in disruption and connections. Faith is a muscle; if we want to grow, we have to exercise.

One of the most difficult transitions for me was *informing people less* and *involving people more*. As Dr. Tim Elmore noted in a blog post on his site, *Growing Leaders*, "shifting from *lecturing* to *facilitating* discoveries is a different mindset, but it's worth the switch. It's less about 'me' delivering and more about 'them' discovering." Dr. Elmore's discovery mirrored mine but transitioning from my dominant *information* process toward an *involvement* process proved hard.[16]

One of the most difficult transitions for me was *informing people less* and *involving people more*.

God gave us the Bible to transform us, not simply inform us. His word should give us a *bigger heart*, not a *bigger head*. As James 2:18 says, "How can you show me your faith if you don't have good deeds? I will show you my faith by my good deeds." (NLT)

His word should give us a *bigger heart*, not a *bigger head*.

Just talking about the need is not enough. Listening to a sermon doesn't naturally equate to action. Releasing people outside the walls of the church requires more than an *explanation*; they need an *experience* where brokenness becomes real, and they find themselves carrying the fullness of Jesus to a wounded and hurting world. Using unfamiliar and culturally different environments stretches people and is valuable in producing life-change. Unless we intentionally place ourselves in uncomfortable experiences, we don't fully rely on God and the power of his Holy Spirit to empower and transform us.

> Releasing people outside the walls of the church requires more than an *explanation*; they need an *experience* where brokenness becomes real.

HOW BROKENNESS SHAPES PASSION AND LEADS TO HUMILITY

Consistently positioning our congregation close to brokenness ignites passion. Why? Because brokenness connects us with God's heart for his people. When we fulfill our calling to be disciples who make disciples wherever they are, we find ourselves face-to-face with broken people. The distance between us and brokenness directly correlates to our passion. The greater the distance, the colder our hearts grow, and the less empathy and passion we have. The smaller the distance between us and brokenness, the more empathy we have, and the more passion compels us to action.

Passion is the fuel behind our faith, propelling us forward when difficulties arise, and we're tempted to quit. Getting next to brokenness helps us confront our own brokenness and enlarges our love and concern for the eternal salvation of others. As Luke 7:47b says, "Whoever has been forgiven little loves little." (NIV) The inverse is also true. Whoever has been forgiven much loves much.

I love what Dr. Brené Brown, author and speaker, says, "… we've divided the world into 'those who need help' and 'those who offer help.' The truth is, we are both."[17]

Until we get next to brokenness, we don't recognize our own poverty of soul. Our brokenness allows us to love authentically and connect with others no matter their situation. Brokenness makes us truly human and empowers us to be image bearers of Christ's love.

FAR FROM EASY

Getting next to brokenness is far from easy. Quite honestly, when I started working in the inner city, I wanted to quit. But I knew I couldn't give up because of a conversation I'd had with God on a night I'll never forget.

That night, I turned onto our street an hour before midnight. Flashing police lights made my heart race. Yellow crime tape marked off the house next to ours. A crowd of people blocked my path. An ominous feeling made the hair on my neck prickle.

Our little neighbor girls had been murdered. My legs buckled underneath me. The girls, friends of my daughters, practically lived at our home and regularly attended Bible club with us. Chloe and Care Bear couldn't be gone.

My own doubts surfaced. The staggering problems of crime and gang violence overwhelmed me. I'd had one car stolen and another ruined when gang initiates put sugar in the engine. *Was our work in the inner city worth the cost of putting my family in danger? Could we really make a difference in lives? Should I give up and quit?*

In the quiet before dawn, I sensed God begin to speak. In the midst of my doubt, fear and confusion, I heard Him engage me in a series of questions.

Ron, remember the neighbor woman across the street? The one who looks 60 even though she's 28?

I thought about the young woman with the vacant expression. Hollow eyes met mine whenever I tried to make conversation. Drugs and prostitution had robbed her of her youth.

Can she leave this community?

"Well, no, Lord, she can't."

What about your neighbor who comes knocking on your door asking for his next fix? He's been addicted to drugs for so long, his mind is virtually gone.

I exhaled. This man could barely string together a coherent thought.

Ron, can he leave this community?

"No." I shook my head, knowing poverty, addiction and circumstances trapped him.

Ron, how about the little girl across the street? You know she's been molested at least three times. You tried to get the police involved, but they said there wasn't enough evidence.

My heart ached at the thought of the sweet eight-year-old trapped in the house of her abuse. The injustice made me want to scream.

Can this abused little girl leave this community?

For the third time, my answer was negative.

I felt God look straight into my eyes. *Then, Ron, neither can you.*

No amount of teaching or preaching could shape me with the level of passion that I carry because of this faith-shaping experience.

Today, I have a murder map hanging in my office which reminds me of the people dying around me without hope. Five bullets I keep in my pocket—all found on our property—are a tangible symbol for me to press on to live each day with a sense of urgency to love and reach people far from Christ. With an impassioned heart, I live "sent" as an everyday missionary, sharing hope in the midst of a messy and broken world.

THE POWER OF DISRUPTION

God isn't asking each of us to move to the inner city, but he is asking each of us to get close to brokenness, so we hurt for what breaks his heart. The real power of brokenness is disruption. Anything that disrupts our daily routines and thought processes positions us for change. Disruption makes us uncomfortable. In our discomfort, we recognize our need for God. Without becoming desperate for God, we have a false sense of control and become self-reliant. Unless we get past ourselves, past our comfort levels, and past the familiar, we will stay in the seats, unchanged and unmoved. That's one of the reasons God has called his disciples to GO!

Getting out of our routine environments and culture is the key to disruption. We must be confronted with the unfamiliar. For each of us, this looks different. Everyone can experience another reality through disruption. For example, when the rich are confronted by poverty, their hearts break for what breaks God's heart. The same is true on the opposite spectrum. People living in poverty often lose the ability to dream. Going on a college visit or visiting another country opens their world to possibilities.

Why is disruption valuable?

One of the dangers of being a Christian is getting comfortable. Getting outside the walls of the church challenges our natural tendency to stagnate. Without tension, we prefer to stay in our comfortable worlds. However, growth occurs when tension unsettles us from staying in the same place. God is comfortable when we're uncomfortable because then we must trust and rely on him.

> God is comfortable when we're uncomfortable because then we must trust and rely on him.

A FAITH-SHAPING, EXPERIENCE-RICH DISCIPLESHIP PLAN

The tension created by disruption challenges us to change. As leaders, we need to incorporate disruption into our discipleship plan and growth strategy. Instead of thinking in terms of another teaching, sermon or Bible study, we need to think in terms of faith-shaping experiences with tension and disruption. Consistently getting people involved in the inner city, prisons, homeless shelters and other cross-cultural, disruptive and unfamiliar places impassions the heart. People gain a different perspective and the ability to empathize when they consistently interact in these types of disruptive environments. In the middle of the messiness, we become equipped to serve like Jesus and make disciples like he did.

> Instead of thinking in terms of another sermon or Bible study, we need to think in terms of experiences with tension and disruption.

Our discipleship plan doesn't need to get better; it needs to get different. Faith-shaping experiences in disruption are the game changer.

An experience-rich discipleship plan is not an option for our congregation. As pastors and church leaders, we must create a consistent pathway for our congregation to be stretched through brokenness. Only then will they grow in their dependence on God. Not only must we teach God's word, we must equip our congregation by giving them consistent formational experiences. Practice must follow information.

> Our discipleship plan doesn't need to get better; it needs to get different.

Faith is not simply built through prayer, sermons and more Bible studies. Getting out of the seats and into the streets adds incredible value in forming powerful disciples who embrace their faith and learn to share the good news with others.

CHAPTER

8

FAITH-SHAPING
CONNECTIONS

PEOPLE-REACHING

Though life in the inner city comes with challenges, Bridge members Keenan and Kiki wouldn't change their environment. Building faith-shaping connections top the list. The family takes leftovers to neighbors in need and gives rides to people during the winter months. When the temperatures soar into the triple digits, they've been known to buy an electric fan for a neighbor or popsicles to share with the neighbor kids.

Keenan and Kiki are one of 34 lighthouse leaders who are following their calling and putting faith into action. Giving our congregation a purpose changed the focus from self to others. We became a church focused on building God's kingdom instead of our empire. At Bridge, we intentionally emphasize developing a purposeful relationship with Jesus by casting a vision for our members to transform their neighborhoods.

> Giving our congregation a purpose changed the focus from self to others.

In Matthew 23:39, Jesus took over six hundred Old Testament commandments and boiled them down to two: love God and love your neighbor as yourself.

What if witnessing is not only a *heart* issue, but an issue of developing *habits* in a Christ-follower? What if, as pastors and church leaders, we could do a much better job of training our congregation as powerful witnessing disciples who make disciples?

Christ-followers don't only need more training time in *Bible study*; we need more training time in *people-reaching*.

> Christ-followers don't only need
> more training time in *Bible study*;
> we need more training time in *people-reaching*.

If I'm going to lead my church, I can't just point to the broken world, and say, "There's your mission field; now go do something." I need to equip my congregation with real-life connections with people far from Christ. People need to be discipled and trained by walking alongside me, observing how I live and share the gospel with others. If I connect with the unchurched, they, too, can be released to do the same.

Engaging with unchurched people from different backgrounds gets the churched out of their comfort levels and intentionally positions them in new relationships. With this deliberate shift, believers continue to grow by forming faith-shaping connections with the unchurched. This new mindset focuses on reaching the lost like missionaries going to another culture abroad.

CONNECTING WITH THE LOST

At Bridge, in addition to loving our neighbors and carrying the fullness of Jesus into where we live, we build faith-shaping connections by loving our neighbors **where there's need** and **where we worship**. Because the latter two are primarily congregation-driven, this allows us to serve together side by side. Loving our neighbors together where there's need disrupts our congregation while loving our neighbors where we worship connects our church with unbelievers. Serving together allows us to practice developing our purposeful relationship with Christ. We not only sharpen one another, we encourage and elevate one another to greater impact.

As churches act as light and salt in engaging their communities, real transformation in Christ happens in both the city and the church. With Bridge, a huge shift occurred when we began to have as much concern for our community as we had for our congregation.

> A huge shift occurs when we have
> as much concern for our community
> as we have for our congregation.

Love outreaches become faith-shaping connections, **connecting the churched with the unchurched** and **training members to be unleashed as powerful witnesses who regularly share their faith.** The following questions help ensure that our outreaches meet both goals.

Connecting with Unbelievers

- Does the love outreach meaningfully engage the unchurched?
- Are we enhancing the community we are serving?
- Do we offer an invitation to visit church?

In addition to impacting the city, successful outreaches must also build and develop the very people doing the outreach. Consistent outreaches give church people opportunities to communicate Christ's love in the city. On-the-job training develops disciples to become saltier and brighter as they share their faith in action.

Questions for Training our Congregation

- Does the love outreach stretch the faith of our congregation?
- Are the churched learning to connect with the unchurched and share their faith?
- Do we train and unleash our members to reach their own neighbors through the love outreach?

We can't expect to get physically fit if we go to the gym once a year. In the same way, we need regular practice and training if we want to get spiritually fit as followers of Jesus who live with a real sense of purpose and calling. We need consistent practice and training to truly love our neighbors, share our faith and grow into the disciple-multiplying disciples Jesus calls us to be.

LOVING OUR NEIGHBORS
WHERE THERE'S NEED

Loving our neighbors **where there's need** is serving the area within your city where people face significant social challenges such as violence, poverty and other disparities. Partnering with an inner-city church to build relationships within the community is a great place to start. This disrupts the congregation out of what's familiar and provides opportunities for church leaders to model and train the church in becoming powerful witnesses. We aren't called to simply offer charity and do something good; we're called to see real kingdom change. Getting involved is the key, adding a depth where real impact is made on both the churched and unchurched. When working toward real change, everyone involved is impacted.

The power of working among brokenness is reciprocal; the very brokenness experienced by the congregation transforms them into humble and compassionate Christ-followers. When brokenness enlarges our hearts to be more like Christ, the fruit of the spirit naturally flows out of us in our daily interactions. We can't help but be transformed. Like short-term missions, these faith-shaping connections should be a consistent part of our discipleship plan.

> These faith-shaping connections should be a consistent part of our discipleship plan.

When extending into an area of need in our city, we need to be sensitive to those we are engaging. Otherwise we come across as patronizing. Building consistent relationships is at the heart of our mission. Sadly, many churches, in their attempt to extend beyond the walls, only address temporal little "c" benevolent causes. These little "c" causes, while helpful, impact a small number of recipients. They are often expensive to administer and don't involve strong relational connections. These benevolent actions touch on the symptoms rather than address the root of the problem or the ultimate suffering of people separated from Christ.

Our world is full of needs, but if we're not careful, we'll get distracted with all kinds of good activity and miss the very mission we're called to fulfill. We've been called to be wise stewards; it's critical that our compassionate and benevolent hearts are Christ-centered and kingdom-advancing.

For years, we had a food pantry that created distance and disempowerment in the very people we tried to help. We quickly learned that our food pantry or any type of outreach best happens when meaningful relationships occur. Further, we want our outreaches to connect people with a local church where they can develop into vibrant disciples of Jesus.

Oftentimes as I consult with churches, I ask pastors what type of outreach they do. Most describe something related to the distribution of food or other one-time benevolent activities. A food pantry is an example of a little "c" cause that can do more harm than good. When we blow in, blow up and blow out without developing consistent relationships with people, we risk: 1. Placing unhealthy relational barriers between the giver and the recipient, and 2. Losing the relational equity needed to share the gospel and plug people into the local church.

While food distribution is important, this good work can be a deterrent to the very relationships we want to form with our neighbors. Benevolent distribution types of ministry are often not mutually reinforcing. Sadly, they oftentimes pit the person of power over the person of need and create an unhealthy relationship.

We've made a rule in our neighborhood strategy that we never want money or resources to get in the way of our relationships. Offering food or other resources happens best once the relationship has been formed and well underway.

In our humanitarian goodness, this seems counter-intuitive, void of compassion. And yet when we respond to the immediate need, rather than let God work, we often miss out on the bigger eternal picture.

For example, we have several homeless individuals that attend our church. One evening during small groups, I sat next to a homeless man who had attended church for six weeks. As I listened, I considered how I once would've approached his situation. My old self would've been quick to provide temporary relief rather than let relationship lead the way. However, I have learned that God often uses our desperation to get our attention and grab our affection. I didn't want to interrupt the process if God wanted to use this man's temporary situation to get his attention. Far too often, our humanitarian hearts get in the way, and we interrupt the very thing that God would use in a life for the greater good.

Living in an area of overwhelming need has shown me that God is the ultimate hope. I can't supply every need and resource, but his supply is limitless. Building relationships with people is key; not only do we point them to the Father, we can help them in tangible ways without fueling an entitlement and enablement mentality.

Though we do provide some resources to show God's goodness, rescuing people from financial poverty is not our primary goal. Far too often our resources have gotten in the way of relationships. Because of the time involved, it can be easier to write a check rather than engage with others. If we're not in a relational journey with people, our resources will only compound the problem and not address spiritual poverty.

As we serve together as a congregation, we can't help but be impacted. Not only do we build relationships with our neighbors in need, our faith is built as we look for opportunities to engage in relational disciple making. God knows exactly how he wants to meet our every need. If we simply trust him, he'll powerfully show up and turn the brokenness into something beautiful. Talk about life-changing.

LOVING OUR NEIGHBORS WHERE WE WORSHIP

Loving our neighbors **where we worship** is serving and connecting with the community surrounding the location of your church building. This is an area of impact where church leaders model what it looks like to extend Christ's love outside the church walls. This is a great training opportunity for the congregation to make faith-shaping connections and practice interacting with unchurched neighbors in a loving way. When we get excited about the life of our church, inviting others becomes less awkward and more natural. We want our neighbors to know the church is a friendly place and available for them.

These larger love outreaches allow everyone in the church to be involved in serving regularly. When we serve together in the same environment, we can engage more unchurched people and make a difference in our community while also training and unleashing our congregation to reach their own neighbors where they live and interact.

When orchestrating a love outreach in the area where you worship, take a *broad* approach and engage as many people as possible. While every person matters, leaders must think about influencing the *broader* number of people in their congregation and community of impact. Reducing our outreach to little "c" *benevolent causes* limits our ability to mobilize our entire congregation and impact the greatest number of people in our surrounding community.

Regular outreaches allow our neighbors to experience the value of our church in the community while inviting them to Sunday morning service. Our prayer is that our churches would be strongly missed if we left the city, and our neighbors would experience the incredible loss because of the practical value we bring to their lives.

> Our prayer is that our churches would be
> strongly missed if we left the city,
> and our neighbors would experience the
> incredible loss because of the
> practical value we bring to their lives.

IDEAS FOR LOVE OUTREACHES

Love outreaches come in a variety of forms. The most effective are those where the cultural inroad builds trust and connection with the largest number of people in our community. By engaging with a broad audience, the church gains social influence which can then translate to spiritual impact.

To appeal to the community around where you worship, four categories of outreach emerge:

- community events
- sports programs
- business outreaches
- school programs

The following chart gives some examples of possible activities we can use to make cultural inroads.

Community Events	Sports Programs
a. Block parties.	a. Select sports programs.
b. Neighborhood clean-up.	b. Recreational teams.
c. Concerts in the park.	c. Parent-involvement
d. Movie nights in the park.	programs. (Father/son or
e. Holiday events.	mother/daughter events.)
f. Fun family activities.	d. Camps. (Invite high level
g. Marriage retreats.	athletes to conduct camps.)
h. Financial classes.	
i. Support groups.	
j. Young moms' groups.	

Business Outreaches	School Programs
a. Coffee Shop.	a. Teacher appreciation days.
b. Kids' attractional activities.	b. Volunteers who read with
c. Counseling center.	students or become
d. Medical clinic.	mentors.
e. Technology center.	c. Tutoring.
	d. Summer camps. (STEM,
	coding, trades/skills)
	e. LEGO-building classes.
	f. Robotics classes.

Imagine doing consistent love outreach activities as a church. Not only is this a powerful training ground for the congregation, conversion growth is the natural outcome when we regularly love the neighbors around where we worship.

The goal is to make a practical difference in the area around your church while inviting your neighbors to visit one of your services. This is the power of social influence that leads to spiritual impact. Neighbors will know your church is a caring, friendly place, adding value to the community.

UNLEASHING DISCIPLES

In John 4, Jesus meets a Samaritan woman at the well who had been married multiple times and lived with someone out of wedlock. Definitely not the most qualified person to lead nearly a whole town to Christ. Yet, in verse 39, John states, "Many of the Samaritans from that town believed in him because of the woman's testimony." (NIV)

Far from the poster child for morality, this woman barely knew enough to share her faith. Yet, she testified how Jesus impacted her life, leading many to believe in the savior of the world.

The same is true for every Christ-follower. Jesus uses willing hearts. While none of us will ever be perfectly qualified, Jesus loves to show up when we are weak. (2 Corinthians 12:10)

Jesus' prayer to see heaven come on earth is our prayer as well. Passionate followers of Christ live the same way, getting out of the seats and into the streets to extend hope to the hopeless. As pastors and leaders, it is up to us to mobilize and extend our congregations outside of the church walls to meet with modern-day tax collectors and sinners.

> Passionate followers of Christ live the same way, getting out of the seats and into the streets to extend hope to the hopeless.

The local church is God's answer for a broken and dying world. Empowering Christians who are willing to share the good news of the gospel unleashes our congregation to extend the hope of Jesus to the lost.

THE LIGHTHOUSE CONCEPT

These simple, yet profound, steps to engage the unchurched grew into a movement at Bridge and its nonprofit partner, Abide. Families moved into targeted inner-city neighborhoods and became lighthouses offering hope through the strategy of connect, care and call.

When we first began, the overwhelming housing problems in the inner city seemed daunting. Over 3,200 properties were considered condemned, abandoned or uninhabitable. When owners didn't maintain their homes, care for the community diminished and crime flourished. Police call this the "broken window" effect because unmaintained neighborhoods and condemned houses become havens for drugs, gangs and violence. Cleaner neighborhoods are safer neighborhoods.

Bridge and Abide targeted two crime-ridden neighborhoods for revitalization. Two houses—just blocks apart—quickly became the focus when we bought the properties. An army of volunteers gutted and remodeled the houses.

Before the transformation, graffiti covered the walls and drug syringes littered the property on Fowler Avenue which had been abandoned for 13 years. This house served as a catalyst for change in the neighborhood. With each improvement, one neighbor after another emerged. Energized by the changes, neighbors began to watch out for each other. Transforming one home impacted the entire neighborhood, creating a new sense of community. The property on Larimore Street mirrored the same effect.

Picking up trash, mowing empty lots, fixing abandoned properties and creating community caused a decrease in crime in these two neighborhoods, and the police took notice. When officers asked the neighbors what happened, they pointed to our home which also housed the church and nonprofit offices.

"We don't know what you're doing," the police told me. "But it's working. Two years ago, this was one of the most dangerous neighborhoods in Omaha. Today, it's one of the safest."

As a result, the lighthouse concept was born.

When the Fowler house neared completion, Bridge recruited and trained a family to live in the lighthouse. As an advocate for the neighborhood, the lighthouse family lived out the three C's of connect, care and call.

The benefits have been priceless. Crime has dropped in these neighborhoods, and residents are empowered to change their neighborhoods and connect with the church in ways they never thought possible.

To date, we have 34 lighthouses and adopted 165 of the 700 neighborhoods. The inner city is being revitalized, people are coming to Christ and disciples are being made.

Getting out of the seats and into the streets is a highly effective training ground to unleash faith. There is power when we serve together as a congregation or shine in our neighborhoods as lighthouses. These faith-shaping connections transform us, making us more Christ-like and empowering us with purpose to advance his kingdom on earth.

CHAPTER

9

DO CHURCH
DIFFERENT

DIFFERENT, NOT BETTER

Christianity is sometimes described as an upside-down kingdom. *If you want to become greatest, you must become a servant. If you want to live, you must die.* These commands show the counter-intuitive nature of Christianity.

In his book, *Good to Great,* Jim Collins argues the enemy of greatness is often the very good you're doing. Improvement isn't enough. Rather, achieving greatness requires a different set of beliefs. Oftentimes, the very actions that move you to greatness are contrary to the good currently being done.[18]

Consider the sport of high jumping. For years, athletes trained tirelessly in jumping higher and higher. They worked on their speed, technique and strength, but only increased their jumping by inches. When Dick Fosbury decided to jump *backwards,* this radically changed everything. The winning jumps increased by feet instead of inches, completely altering the sport of high jumping.

What if the *good* things we're doing in ministry keep us from accomplishing *great* things? What if *getting better* means doing *church different?"*

> What if getting better means doing *church different?*

After 30 years of ministry, I've found that cutting-edge solutions are not found in doing *church better.*

We must do **church different.**

DeAngelo

He stood out. Everywhere DeAngelo went, he drew stares because of the tattoos covering every inch of his face and body. Despite growing up in church, DeAngelo never fit in. Depressed and struggling with an undiagnosed mental illness, DeAngelo turned to gang activity and drugs. His choices eventually landed him in jail.

Soon after finishing his sentence, DeAngelo played with his eight kids at the park when one of our pastors struck up a conversation and invited him to Bridge. Desperate to find a job and a new start, the opportunity to be surrounded by people with similar backgrounds who could point him to hope intrigued him.

When DeAngelo and his family came to Bridge, they encountered a multi-ethnic church where businessmen and professionals sat beside people with a history of gang activity and drug abuse. The curious stares he usually received were replaced by a church family who accepted him just the way he was.

DeAngelo felt loved and began to have hope that his life could mean something. Another pastor even promised to help him find a job. DeAngelo gave his life to Christ and began a faith journey of his own. Still navigating the ups and downs of leaving his old life of drugs behind, DeAngelo is getting help and growing as a loving husband and father. He still receives stares, but now DeAngelo is eager to share how God has transformed his life and wants to do the same for others.

SHAWN

Shawn grew up going to church with his mother, but the men in his life were physically abusive alcoholics who never attended church. Figuring Christianity meant being nice and good, Shawn left the church as a teenager because he felt more moral than most of the kids in his youth group. He dropped out of college multiple times and left several jobs in a futile attempt to find fulfillment through the American dream.

I met Shawn several years ago and invited him to church. Bridge flipped Shawn's world upside down as he encountered a church filled with hope and purpose. He and his wife, Jodi, immediately felt at home.

Shawn surrendered his life to Christ, and with discipleship, discovered God's call on his life. He and

Jodi are now lighthouse leaders who help others find hope and purpose. They are everyday missionaries.

When we do *church different*, people encounter the powerful presence of Jesus who wants to have a personal and purposeful relationship with each of his followers. DeAngelo and Shawn are great examples of the transformation that God intends when his church demonstrates love-hope-faith.

A NEW CULTURE

The early church didn't stay confined behind closed doors. And neither should we.

As Rodney Stark wrote in *The Rise of Christianity*, "Christianity served as a revitalization movement that arose in response to the misery, chaos, fear, and brutality of life in the urban Greco-Roman world . . . To cities filled with the homeless and the impoverished, Christianity offered charity as well as hope. To cities filled with newcomers and strangers, Christianity offered an immediate basis for attachments. To cities filled with orphans and widows, Christianity provided a new and expanded sense of family. To cities torn by violent ethnic strife, Christianity offered a new basis for social solidarity. And to cities faced with epidemics, fires, and earthquakes, Christianity offered effective nursing services . . . For what they brought was not simply an urban movement, but a new culture." [19]

Can the church impact our culture in America today?

The task seems daunting. Impossible even. The size of the problems can overwhelm us until fear and doubt paralyze us.

But we're not alone. God never meant for us to be a solo act. He gave us the church because we're better and stronger together. The church is the beginning point on the mobilization flywheel. As it turns, the biblical and disciple-making church makes everyday missionaries who birth new gatherings and churches and ultimately, a new flywheel where the process begins all over again.

MOVING PEOPLE FROM HERE TO THERE

Before becoming a pastor, I worked as a chemical engineer and served as an elder in one of the largest churches in Omaha. I taught Bible study classes and led outreaches where over 200 people joined me to serve and evangelize. My pastor noted my success in rallying people together and asked to meet. Expecting to discuss leadership strategies, his question surprised me.

"With such a large following, where are you taking them?"

Wow. What a question.

I'd never considered the idea of taking people anywhere. I just did church—or what I considered church to be. Go to Sunday morning service. Pray. Study the Bible. Serve. Not once did I think about the need for a road map to help people move toward a purposeful relationship in Christ.

When I became a pastor years later, this question transformed the way I saw the role of leadership within the church.

I needed to take my congregation somewhere. I needed a big picture—an outline.

The love-hope-faith revelation gave me a blueprint to take my congregation from here to there.

DEMONSTRATE LOVE

Start by demonstrating love. When we increase our social influence, we will have incredible spiritual impact. As we pursue a purposeful relationship with Jesus, we focus less on ourselves and become more aware of others. Focusing on others outside the walls of the

186

church increases our cultural IQ and grows our heart and empathy for the hurting and broken around us. A sense of urgency wells inside us as we long for our co-workers, our neighbors and the lost in our community to experience the same hope we've found in Jesus.

The church which infiltrates and engages the community on a consistent basis through love outreaches heightens social influence, sensitivity and awareness in its members. By serving and loving our neighbors together where we worship and where there's need, we begin to extend this same love into our own neighborhoods where we live using the practical strategy of connect, care, call. Loving our neighbors compels us to change our scorecard as we keep engaged with unbelievers and stay ready to share our hope.

INSPIRE HOPE

When pastors and leaders develop cultural inroads into the community, their congregation becomes consistently involved with unbelievers. As relationships form through loving engagement with neighbors, inspiring hope is the next step. So, what does hope look like?

Without understanding the difference between good works and God's work, we can get so caught up in providing temporary hope that we miss eternal hope.

Helping meet physical needs is important but not at the expense of losing a soul. The church and the centrality of the gospel must be at the heart of inspiring hope. Only then can lives find real transformation and behavioral change.

Transformation is a messy process. The church must embrace the mess and be sensitive and welcoming to all guests. Intentionally building a culture of hope is critical to retaining guests week after week. Making a few key changes can make or break the newcomer's experience. Sunday mornings become an opportunity to stretch our faith and expect God to show up in powerful ways.

UNLEASH FAITH

Sermons and Bible studies alone don't produce disciples. Faith is shaped by cultivating opportunities for connection with unbelievers and experiences in disruption. When God breaks our hearts for what breaks his heart, we don't stagnate, and faith comes alive. Getting uncomfortable shapes powerful disciples who unleash their faith and share the good news with others.

Leadership must drive all three—love, hope and faith—if we're going to do *church different* and reach people far from Christ. Without placing leaders at the helm, there is no direction. Leaders must be empowered to direct love outreaches, build a culture of hope on Sunday mornings, and develop faith in their disciples by showing them how to share the gospel amidst disruption while connecting with unbelievers.

THE POWER OF LOVE-HOPE-FAITH

The spiritual gets practical when Christians get out of the seats. And the practical turns powerful when Christians get into the streets and make a difference in the world around them, being disciples who make disciples wherever they go. Gaining social influence is critical to our ongoing ability to have spiritual impact.

A church with a heart of love-hope-faith is tireless in its pursuit to make cultural inroads to see lives and cities transformed by the powerful love of Jesus.

Our neighbors in every part of our city are desperate for hope. As pastors and leaders, we lead the charge. We bear the privilege and responsibility for sharing the good news in our generation. We must lead the church to . . .

- **DEMONSTRATE LOVE** to unbelievers.

- **INSPIRE HOPE** in the church with the unchurched in mind.

189

- **UNLEASH FAITH** in God's people to impact a lost and broken world.

What would be the impact across America if the church got out of the seats and into the streets?

Imagine consistent love outreaches igniting God's people with passion for the lost.

Picture churches brimming with guests because Sunday mornings elevate and inspire hope.

How would regular faith-shaping experiences with disruption and connections with the lost unleash world-changing disciples to impact a broken world?

My prayer is that God will lead your church in becoming different, changing the world through the principles of love, hope, and faith.

What got us here won't get us there. It's time to change.

Together, let's do *church different*.

Section III:
UNLEASH FAITH

Key Concept: Because we are more formed than informed, preaching and teaching are not enough in our discipleship plan. We must form disciples through regular experiences in brokenness, disruption and faith-shaping connections.

Commitments:

1. Commit to regular experiences in disruption by creating a consistent pathway for your congregation to be stretched through brokenness.
2. Regularly make faith-shaping connections with the lost by serving together as a congregation where you worship and where there's need.
3. Do church *different* not better . . . demonstrate love, inspire hope and unleash faith.

Questions:

1. What does it mean that we are more formed than informed?

2. As a leader, how can you *inform people less* and *involve people more*?

3. What is the benefit to your congregation to have regular faith-shaping experiences in brokenness and disruption?

4. How can you develop faith-shaping connections with the lost by loving your neighbors where you worship and where there's need?

5. Is your church experiencing conversion growth? Why or why not?

6. How do you unleash faith in God's people to impact a broken world?

7. Revisit your initial understanding of love-hope-faith. How do you understand the revelation now?

HOW TO SHARE
YOUR CONVERSION STORY

Many Christians feel inadequate or freeze when they are asked to share their conversion story. Fear and confusion often keep believers from sharing the greatest treasure in their lives.

A popular radio host and proclaimed atheist didn't take offense when a listener gave him a Bible. When asked why, he responded that if you believed Jesus was the only way to heaven, you would have to absolutely hate someone NOT to share your hope.[20]

Wow.

Many believers don't know where to start or what to say.

As leaders, we need to help Christ-followers process and practice sharing their conversion stories. Consider *before* and *after* pictures on make-over shows or diet commercials. As Christians, we also have a *before* and *after* picture.

At Bridge, we encourage believers to **process** and **practice** sharing their conversion stories in the following 3-step process.

Step 1. Choose three words/phrases that best describe your life without Christ at the center. Many people have a spiritual perception and believe that God is *important*. While this sensitivity, along with a connection to church is helpful, becoming a Christian has a decisive starting point. Choosing to turn away from our self-motivated plans and self-focused lifestyle in order to place Jesus at the *center* of our lives is where real change takes place.

When Christ becomes central in our lives, everything we do revolves around His dreams and plans for our lives. Instead of God or church being another important thing in our life, we deliberately build our entire lifestyle, plans and future around the ways of Jesus. Rather than *run our own lives*, we are now *under new management*, where we commit to following God's plans for the rest of our lives. Jesus becomes *the boss* of our lives, and we live to love, obey and fulfill His purpose.

Examples:
- EMPTY—I felt empty and alone.
- DRUGS—I was addicted to drugs.
- PURPOSE—I had no purpose in my life.

Step 2. Choose three words/phrases that best describe your life at the time you surrendered to Jesus. How did God use this circumstance(s) to get your attention and eventually your affection?

Examples:

- ACCIDENT—I almost died in a car accident. Thinking about death really got my attention, and I decided to surrender the control of my life and follow Jesus.
- DRUNK—I woke up with a hangover and knew there had to be more to life. Empty and depressed, I gave my life to Jesus.
- BROTHER—My brother became a Christian, and I saw how he changed. I wanted the same, so I repented, asked God to forgive me, and invited Jesus to come into my life.

Step 3. Choose three words/phrases that best describe what Christ is doing in your life today. What is God doing, that you could never do on your own, that reveals His love and power? Make sure to give practical, concrete words/phrases to describe the change.

Examples:

- I SMILE MORE—I am so hopeful for my future. Suicide is not the answer. I have so much joy. Every day is a gift I want to share with others.
- CLEAN AND SOBER—I'm no longer addicted to alcohol and drugs, and I'm helping others find freedom as well.
- I LOVE SHARING MY FAITH—My life has meaning now, and I want others to find hope

and purpose, too. I talk with people regularly about how God changed my life.

At Bridge, our discipleship training begins the moment someone says "yes" to Jesus. During our baptism class, we challenge people to share their conversion story with three people. Extending and witnessing God's love to others begins on day one.

Notes

Introduction
1. Malphurs, Aubrey. The Malphurs Group. "The State of the American Church: Plateaued or Declining." *http://malphursgroup.com/state-of-the-american-church-plateaued-declining/*
2. Ibid.
3. Eaton, Sam. "12 Reasons Millennials Are Over Church." *https://www.recklesslyalive.com/12-reasons-millennials-are-over-church/* Recklessly Alive. September 29, 2016.

Chapter 2
4. Polling & Analysis. "'Nones' on the Rise." *http://www.pewforum.org/2012/10/09/nones-on-the-rise/* Pew Research Center. Oct. 9, 2012.
5. Demographic Study. "America's Changing Religious Landscape." *http://www.pewforum.org/2015/05/12/chapter-3-demographic-profiles-of-religious-groups/* Pew Research Center. May 12, 2015.
6. Denison, Jim. The Daily Article. "Why is today's Senate hearing so crucial?" *https://mailchi.mp/denisonforum/why-is-todays-senate-hearing-so-crucial?e=9057537402* Denison Forum. September 27, 2018.
7. Photo by Sanjeewa Wickramasekera used by permission.

8. Noonan, Peggy. "Trump, Sanders and the American Rebellion." *http://www.peggynoonan.com/trump-sanders-and-the-american-rebellion/* The Wall Street Journal. February 18, 2016.

9. "Barth in Retirement." *http://content.time.com/time/subscriber/article/0,33009,896838,00.html* Time. May 31, 1963.

Chapter 4

10. Frankl, Viktor. *Man's Search for Meaning.* Beacon Press, 1946.

Chapter 5

11. Rainer, Thom. "Six Reasons Why Your Church Members May Not Be Friendly to Guests." *https://thomrainer.com/2016/09/six-reasons-church-members-may-not-friendly-guests/* Growing Healthy Churches Together. Sept. 19, 2016.

12. BBC News. "'One in 10' Attends Church Weekly." *http://news.bbc.co.uk/2/hi/uk_news/6520463.stm* April 3, 2007.

13. Warren, Rick. "11 Simple Strategies for Helping Guests Feel Welcome." *https://pastors.com/11-simple-strategies-for-helping-guests-fee-welcome* September 25, 2018.

Chapter 6

14. "Rainer's Four Legs of Assimilation." *http://28nineteen.com/rainers-four-legs-of-assimilation/* 28nineteen: All About Disciple-Making. July 31, 2008.

15. Hawkins, Greg L. and Cally Parkinson. *Move: What 1,000 Churches Reveal about Spiritual Growth*. Grand Rapids, Michigan: Zondervan. Willow Creek Association, 2011. 113,120. Print.

Chapter 7

16. Elmore, Tim. "Why One University is Eliminating Lectures." *https://growingleaders.com/blog/why-one-university-eliminating-lecture/* Growing Leaders. November 15, 2016.

17. Brown, Brené. *https://www.goodreads.com/quotes/726129-one-of-the-greatest-barriers-to-connection-is-the-cultural* Goodreads.

Chapter 9

18. Collins, Jim. *Good to Great: Why Some Companies Make the Leap and Others Don't*. Harper Business, 2001.

19. Stark, Rodney. *The Rise of Christianity*. Princeton University Press, 1996, p. 161.

20. McAdams, Keenan. "What Atheist Penn Jillette Taught Me about Evangelism." *http://www.radicallychristian.com/what-atheist-penn-jillette-taught-me-about-evangelism* Radically Christian. March 24, 2013.

Better Together

Thank you for reading *Church Different: Unleashing the Church to Change the World*. After many years of work in the inner city, I feel compelled to share the hard-fought lessons I've learned.

As a fellow pastor, I salute you for your often thankless efforts in leading others. With this heart, I want to encourage you to think differently about church and press on toward the dream of seeing every person, in every neighborhood, have every opportunity to experience and embrace Jesus.

For more information, visit www.outoftheseats.com or download your copy of *Out of the Seats and Into the Seats* on Amazon today. I would love to connect. Message me on Facebook @rondotzlerauthor or Twitter @dotzler_ron.

May God bless you, as together, we join with Christ in doing ***Church Different***!

Ron Dotzler

Acknowledgments

Church Different: Unleashing the Church to Change the World is a compilation of insights and stories behind the success Bridge Church has had in reaching people far from Christ. This impact would not have been possible without the tireless and sacrificial efforts of staff, board members, pastors, friends and thousands of volunteers who have shaped Bridge. Your efforts have made this dream of a different church come true. Together, we are providing hope to countless lives.

I want to especially thank my wife, Twany, for stepping out in faith and persevering when all odds seemed stacked against us. Your encouragement, devotion and faithful disposition have been heart-warming and spirit-lifting. I am so much better because of you. I love you.

I want to thank Josh Dotzler, my son, for your faithful obedience and tenacity in leading the team of Bridge over the past several years. You and Jen have pursued Christ without wavering, as reflected in your humility and leadership. As a young bi-racial leader, your zeal and wisdom have built an incredibly diverse team that is accomplishing great things in our city. Thank you for consistently working through and walking out the concepts in this book. Whether working late nights or early mornings, your fervor to advance God's kingdom is transforming our city in unprecedented ways. Not only are you leading a movement, this book would never have come to fruition without your love and gifted leadership. May God's richest blessings be yours as you inspire hope amidst despair and destruction. You are truly a man after God's own heart. I love you, Josh and Jen.

I want to thank Myron Pierce, and his wife, Kristin, for obeying Christ through incredible challenges. Knowing your background was nothing short of hopeless, your risk-taking faith inspires others to do great things for God. Your spirit-empowered walk with Christ is a blessing to me and the many you influence. As a young African-American leader in our city, you raise the bar of faith and display a level of reconciliation that is powerful. May God encourage you to press forward to see his kingdom come, his will be done, on earth as it is in heaven. I love you, Myron and Kristin.

A very special thank you to Shawn Deane, my assistant, and Angela Prusia, my ghostwriter. Without your help, the concepts and chapters would not have been as clear or impactful. Words cannot express my gratitude.

I want to thank family and friends who helped advance Bridge. In the early days when I had no idea how to communicate the vision or develop the principles contained in this book, you stuck by me and helped grow Bridge to what it is today.

A very special thanks to Greg and Nancy Thrasher, Paul and Sarah Ludacka, Chuck and Judy Downey, Bob and Joanne Gjere, Dean Hodges, John and Wende Kotouc, Marcus and Sarah Wagstaff, Chris Held, Cindi and the late Doug Jasa, Ray and Jan Dotzler, Dave and Sandi Dotzler, Joe and Barb Dotzler, Jim Blazek, Scott and Alexi Wellman, and Kyle and Karen Anderson. I can't begin to express my gratitude to each of you. If ever there is an award for "game changers," you all would take top prize. When we faced incredible obstacles and challenges, your faithful commitment to making a difference never subsided. I am humbled by your love, friendship and support.

I'll forever be grateful to Larry and Barb Welchert, Don and Catherine Stein, Rick and Renee Berry, and Brad and Julie Knutson. When Twany and I were at our lowest, you were always there.

Special pastors in my life include: Elmer Murdoch, Les Beauchamp, Lincoln Murdoch, the late Ty Schenzel, Pam and the late George Moore, James and Suzanne Patterson, Walter and Melba Hooker, David Witkop and Mark Ashton. I never tire of thanking God for you and telling others of your influence as you bring Christ's kingdom on earth as it is in heaven.

Thank you everyone.

We truly are better together.

Made in the USA
Lexington, KY
16 November 2019